ROUTLEDGE LIBRARY EDITIONS:
HUMAN RESOURCE MANAGEMENT

Volume 36

PLANNING CONTINUING
PROFESSIONAL DEVELOPMENT

PLANNING CONTINUING PROFESSIONAL DEVELOPMENT

Edited by
FRANKIE TODD

Routledge
Taylor & Francis Group

LONDON AND NEW YORK

First published in 1987 by Croom Helm Ltd

This edition first published in 2017
by Routledge
2 Park Square, Milton Park, Abingdon, Oxon OX14 4RN

and by Routledge
711 Third Avenue, New York, NY 10017

Routledge is an imprint of the Taylor & Francis Group, an informa business

© 1987 Frankie Todd

British Library Cataloguing in Publication Data
A catalogue record for this book is available from the British Library

ISBN: 978-1-138-80870-6 (Set)
ISBN: 978-1-315-18006-9 (Set) (ebk)
ISBN: 978-1-138-28720-4 (Volume 36) (hbk)
ISBN: 978-1-138-28722-8 (Volume 36) (pbk)

Publisher's Note
The publisher has gone to great lengths to ensure the quality of this reprint but points out that some imperfections in the original copies may be apparent.

Disclaimer
The publisher has made every effort to trace copyright holders and would welcome correspondence from those they have been unable to trace.

Planning Continuing Professional Development

Edited by
FRANKIE TODD

CROOM HELM
London • New York • Sydney

© 1987 Frankie Todd
Croom Helm Ltd, Provident House, Burrell Row,
Beckenham, Kent, BR3 1AT

Croom Helm Australia, 44-50 Waterloo Road,
North Ryde, 2113, New South Wales

British Library Cataloguing in Publication Data

Published in the USA by
Croom Helm
in association with Methuen, Inc.
29 West 35th Street
New York, NY 10001

British Library Cataloguing in Publication Data

Planning continuing professional development.
 —(New patterns of learning series)
 1. Continuing education. 2. Professional
 education
 I. Todd, Frankie II. Series
 374′.013 LC5215

 ISBN 0-7099-4326-1

Library of Congress Cataloging-in-Publication Data

Planning continuing professional development.

 (New patterns of learning series)
 1. Professional education — Great Britain.
2. Continuing education — Great Britain. I. Todd, Frankie.
II. Series.
LC1072.C56P57 1987   374′.941   87-554
ISBN 0-7099-4326-1

Printed and bound in Great Britain
by Billings & Sons Limited, Worcester.

ACKNOWLEDGEMENTS

The editor would like to acknowledge the patient support given by Angela Fairclough during the preparation of this collection.

CONTENTS

CONTENTS

INTRODUCTION

> Professional development is something that
> occurs where a professional sees his task
> in a new light. I believe this can be
> brought about when outsiders become
> insiders and get involved ... with
> colleagues in their professional job ...
> (Coles, 1977)

> Education should not be seen as an activity
> separated from work but as an integral part
> of the career development of individuals.
> (Williams, 1977)

One of the striking features of late twentieth
century industrialised society is the influential
role of professions and professionals. Most of the
arenas of our lives from birth to death are also
arenas for professional practice: the place and
manner of our birth; our schooling and higher
education; the health care we receive; the
buildings we inhabit and use; the planned features
of our environment; our modes of transport and the
structures of our roads and bridges; our encounters
with the law; our acts of violence and depression;
our ownership and transfer of property; our
bereavements and finally our deaths – in each of
these experiences we are likely to find ourselves
the objects of professional practice.

Professional influence is exerted upon our lives at
different levels. At the national level much
detailed policy making is put out from central and
local government to committees, working parties,
consultative groups and governing bodies upon which
appropriate professions will be represented. Quite
properly, therefore, professionals take part in
making policies which guide the working of some of
our major institutions: schools, the health
service, the legal system. Influence on policy
making is also directly exercised at a national

1

level by professional bodies, as for instance, via lobbying parliament, government departments and ministers. At the local level professionals are involved in managerial and policy decisions which may be made outside democratic machinery. The decision of a GP to set up an anti-smoking clinic; of a social worker to seek black foster parents for black children; of a teacher to order new teaching materials that do not contain gender stereotypes; of a hospital consultant about which categories of patients should take priority for expensive operations where resources are limited: these are all examples of smaller scale policy decisions which professionals may take independently by virtue of the roles they hold.

Beyond all these are decisions about actions in particular cases. Should this elderly confused lady be found a place in an old people's home or should she be given support to live independently? Should this disruptive girl be excluded from school in the knowledge that her home life is such that she may wander the streets? Should this arthritic patient be recommended a drug that radically improves mobility but carries a small risk of serious side-affects? The influence of professional decisions made at this level is perhaps the easiest to identify because these decisions are made about us, or about our relations and friends – they affect our lives in ways that we experience directly.

Professions and professionals, therefore, are everywhere. Upon occasion it is literally our lives that are in their hands, but in many less dramatic instances it is our money, our time or the quality of our lives that reflects the outcomes of professional practice.

This all-pervading influence of professionals is one of the starting points for the work discussed in this collection. For if professional practice can affect our lives in such important ways it follows that the continuing development of these professionals is a key issue for us all. We want to be sure that our dentist understands the differential risks of the use of general and local anaesthetics; that our accountant is up to date on the latest revisions to income tax legislation; that the doctor we encounter in casualty is fully conversant with resuscitation techniques; that our child's teacher is well prepared to teach a new syllabus. If continuing professional development can affect what professionals do it can affect what professionals do to us. From this perspective the book should have some value for the general reader who is interested to find out just how white-coated and be-suited 'experts' go about maintaining their competence. This collection of papers documents some of the considerable effort that goes on, behind the scenes, to maintain good practice standards.

Currently many professional bodies, institutions and employers offer programmes of continuing development for their practitioners. Teachers, doctors, nurses, architects and engineers are some of the groups that come to mind, and all are discussed in this collection. Additionally, in the United Kingdom, the Open Tech, the DES's PICKUP (professional, industrial and commercial up-dating) programmes and the National Health Service's massive investment in training are examples of major national initiatives that cut across specific practitioner groupings. These developments are paralleled in the United States (Houle, 1980) with the additional feature there that continuing participation in learning is commonly compulsory for continued professional registration - a trend which is also becoming more marked in the United Kingdom.

There are, therefore, quite large numbers of people whose job it is to design, organise and implement programmes of continuing education for professionals. This book is aimed at all of these people - whether trained 'trainers' or practitioners who find themselves with a training responsibility - in addition to thoughtful practitioners themselves.

At this point an apology is in order to those readers who like to commence a work armed with a clear set of definitions of terms. There will be no consideration here of the criteria which an occupational grouping should be deemed to satisfy if it wants to call itself a profession; and no roll call of those groups considered to be ´in´ and those thought to be ´out´. There are already other useful discussions of these issues (Houle, 1980; Goodlad, 1984; Jarvis, 1983). The Oxford English Dictionary offers a sufficiently disparate set of definitions to provide ample shelter for tolerant ecumenicism and I suspect my fellow authors would join me in finding the issue of a precise definition an irrelevance, particularly because this terrain is forever shifting.

Nevertheless it is important to note that the relatively innocent view of the professions offered by Carr-Saunders(1928) (in which a profession "may perhaps be defined as an occupation based upon specialised intellectual study and training, the purpose of which is to apply skilled service or advice to others for a definite fee or salary") has been overtaken by others which offer a considerably more cynical view of the way professions may turn their knowledge into power (Ilich, 1977; Freidson, 1970). Equally pertinent are views of professionalism which emphasise the use of expert knowledge to support informed choice by a client (Goodlad, 1984; Schon, 1983).

In this context it is the term "continuing professional development" (CPD) that is the important one and it has come to be used in ways which transcend the definitions of each of its constituent parts. For some time there seemed to be as many ways of referring to continuing education for professionals as there are professional groups. Each has had its own term: "continuing formation" for engineers (Cannell, 1982): "continuing medical education"(CME) for doctors (Bouhuijs, this volume; Rogers, 1982): in-service education for teachers (INSET) (DES, 1972) and so on.

In the mid-1970s Dick Gardner, then Director of the York Centre for the development of continuing education for the building professions sought a term which would convey that "there is more to ´continuing education´ than attendance on courses –

important though those are" (Gardner, 1978). He wanted a term that would not suggest a divide between "education" and "practice" and that would not devalue informal or incidental learning in the course of practice. The phrase continuing professional development offers a context "within which the purely educational element becomes one alongside others; a full professional life, good practice generally, career advancement, increasing capacity and well-earned profit (or its equivalent). Professional development seems to suggest these things and to imply positive learning strategies for individuals, practising organisations, individual professions ..." (Gardner,1978, pp. 2-3).

Continuing professional development therefore conveys an activity that should be thought of as a continuing process rather than something achieved with initial qualification; that members of any group that thinks of itself as professional should engage in it; and it makes no preconceptions about whether people learn or are taught, or about the formality of learning activities. People can develop themselves; others can also help them develop; the important thing is that professional development occurs.

The term (and its useful short form "CPD") has been found sufficiently helpful to be used far beyond its initial constituency and this general acceptance makes it a good phrase to use in this collection. Those readers who take more orthodox views of what a "profession" is could perhaps mentally substitute the word "practitioner" throughout (of course, having defined it properly first!).

The generality of the term CPD reflects a major concern of the collection to discuss general issues relating to the design and implementation of professional development. Those of us who work as facilitators and designers of CPD sometimes seem to over-identify with our client grouping. We talk about "our" architects, nurses, doctors or teachers in much the same way that anthropologists refer to the people they have studied as "my tribe". The

implication is that there is something special –
even exotic – about this group which, because of
our experience of working with them, we happen to
know and understand.

It is natural that we should value hard-won
insider´s knowledge and we must not fail to respond
to significant idiosyncrasies where these exist.
But if we primarily approach each client grouping
as if it has important mysteries that separate it
out from other professional groups, then we deny
ourselves a most powerful cognitive strategy,
namely the capacity to generalise.

My feeling is that approaches to CPD for many
professions suffer from being too local, too
separatist, too idiosyncratic – and therefore too
fragmented. One aim for this collection is to step
back a pace and engage with some of the problems
and possibilities that face everyone involved in
the design and implementation of CPD. The task of
designing and evaluating good practitioner
education is not an easy one and there is a great
deal to be gained from the consideration of methods
and solutions across a range of professions and
providers. As Cyril Houle(1980) has suggested,
"Important consequences follow from the abandonment
of the idea that the learning processes of each
profession are wholly unique."

What is certainly not unique to each profession is
the realisation that CPD can be more effective if
it is planned for the job it has to do. In many
organisations CPD participation occurs on an
entirely ad hoc basis, with correspondingly patchy
results (Todd, 1985). No criteria are set down as
to what CPD should be trying to achieve.

Three features that characterise such an unplanned
approach are (a) that participation in CPD is the
result of arbitrary, top-of-the-head decisions
without reference to any principled evaluation of
what CPD is necessary, (b) that no records of
participation are kept, so there is no way of
knowing afterwards what a CPD "programme" was made
up of, and (c) nevertheless people participate in
CPD events of one kind or another – particularly if

the venue is attractive - and so resources of time
and money are spent on CPD which may have no useful
effects whatsoever - and which subsequently is not
even remembered as having occurred.

Sometimes the totally unplanned approach outlined
above is replaced by what can be called the
"shopping-list" approach where a professional sets
out a forward listing of areas in which to
undertake CPD in the future. Here at least we see a
setting of priorities, and perhaps some attempt to
match CPD participation to the time and money that
are available for it.

But CPD is not a fringe activity; it is one of the
most important resources a professional can draw on
to maintain competence. It is not enough to pick
topics off the lists in the promotional materials
sent out by CPD providers. Rather, CPD needs to be
planned round strategic concerns that link CPD to
evaluations of practice and to analyses of
forthcoming practice demands. This concern for
planning CPD runs right through the collection but
rather than offering a single prescription the
chapters illustrate different approaches to CPD
planning that may be appropriate in different
circumstances.

The emphasis on planning CPD is tightly linked to
another starting point for this collection, namely
the concern that CPD should have the ultimate aim
of enhancing practice. This brings into the arena
criteria for the success of CPD that are different
from - and harder to meet than - those that pertain
to initial training.

An important aim in most courses in higher
education is the promotion of understanding of a
particular body of knowledge; success is measured
in terms of the results of formal assessment
procedures. Attitudinal, experiential and
process-based aims may be added on to this, as for
instance the encouragement of disciplined enquiry,
autonomous learning or practical skills. However,
where a performance-based element is included it is
rarely more than a slimmish part of the whole
sandwich, and takes place within a supervised

setting that protects both student and client from much that could follow in the way of real-life consequences.

By contrast in continual professional education (where it is less common to use any formal means of assessment of learning) the development of new understandings, new attitudes and new skills is a step on the way towards the primary requirement that what is learned should improve work practice. In other words if CPD is to be judged successful it should ideally satisfy two criteria: (a) that learning occurs and (b) that the learning is implemented to the benefit of practice standards. Otherwise there seems little justification for the investment of time and money that CPD programmes require.

However, CPD does not necessarily have good effects on practice. Cyril Houle(1980, p.8) has commented on the "failure of continued study to achieve an adequate adjustment of the requirements of practice". To explain this failure it is helpful to draw a distinction between what a professional knows (competence), what a professional does (performance) and what a professional achieves (effectiveness). It is relatively easy to affect what a professional knows (although human memory and forgetting being what they are it should be borne in mind that effects may be transitory). It is less easy to affect what a professional does with what s/he knows; attitudes, preconceptions and prejudices may all combine to produce little change in action terms from new knowledge and understandings. Bandura(1982) has commented that " ... people often do not behave optimally, even though they know full well what to do." Another commentator has said of medical care " ... most deficiences in care have been shown to result from the poor appliction of knowledge rather than the lack of knowledge ... "(Hanniford, 1981). Arguris and Schön(1974) use the terms "Espoused theories of action" and "theories in use" to examine this frequently found inconsistency between what practitioners say they are doing and what they actually do.

It is even more difficult to affect what a professional achieves for this is influenced by a range of complicated contextual features: patients who fail to follow advice; students who do not do their assignments; managers who refuse to implement new procedures; colleagues who fail to understand them; payment systems that reward less effective but traditional practices. All of these factors mean there can be no simple input-output model for CPD and practice standards.

The main difficulty in designing CPD to enhance practice can be expressed in a simple question: how would we know if it had done so? One way to answer this question would be first to define what is meant by good practice so as to set a standard; then to collect data on existing standards of practice so as to establish where deficiencies in practice occur; then to put on a CPD programme whose content was targeted on these deficiences; then, after some appropriate period, to repeat the collection of data and compare practice standards "after" with those "before".

At this point a critic might draw our attention to some totally extraneous factor occurring during the same time period which might itself have produced the good effects. The practitioners we are looking at might be the products of an improved initial training scheme, for instance, or a major public awareness campaign may have changed clients' behaviours. We might then decide to improve our research design by using a control group of professionals who do not receive the CPD programme and we would assume that if the "CPD receivers" showed more practice improvements than the "non-CPD receivers" then it must be the CPD programme that had made the difference. But we could still be mistaken. Cohen and Manyon (1980) review several sources of threat to the validity of such quasi-experimental research designs conducted in field settings. One problem, for instance, is that the researcher has no way of judging the accuracy of the records on practice actions - inaccurate records may give misleading results.

Despite these difficulties, two professions in particular have been the subjects of detailed researches which have attempted to evaluate practice standards and to explore the relationship between quality outcomes and CPD, and this experience provides some useful insights.

The Medical Audit has focused on the quality of patient care provided by hospital physicians. Hanniford(1981) notes that the methods developed to conduct audits of medical care began by focusing on outcomes (for example, fatalities, disabilities, patients discharged as "cured"), then shifted to considering processes (for example, patient satisfaction, quality of communications between doctor and patient) and then went back to outcomes because of the methodological problems of process-based studies. Most recent strategies use a combination of process and outcome criteria which are locally defined within an individual hospital and with data collection designed around the hospital's system of record keeping. She notes, however, that such a locally based approach produces recommendations for CPD which are relevant only to that hospital's staff. Additionally, medical records do not record all aspects of care given to the patient but primarily reflect technical interventions.

As developed at the Continuing Professional Education Development Project at Pennsylvania State University the Medical Audit has seven stages. These are:

(1) Topic selection.
(2) Adoption of criteria.
(3) Determining the range for each standard.
(4) Data collection using patients' medical records.
(5) Review of the data by a quality assurance committee.
(6) Corrective action.
(7) A re-audit, of major problem areas in practice within a year, of minor ones perhaps after two to three years.

A similar set of stages is shared by most "medical audit" researches.

The appropriate "corrective action" may not always be education. Hanniford cites studies which show other forms of action to be equally or more effective in achieving a desired outcome. Some of these measures manifest an inspired simplicity. For instance, using removable fluorescent tape to obscure abnormal test results from routine screening (the tape was put on in the laboratory) was a better trigger of appropriate follow-up action by doctors than workshops or newsletter reminders (Williamson et al., 1967, cited Hanniford, 1981). One way to improve the efficiency of CPD, therefore, must be to choose appropriate targets, and not to try to use educaton where executive action would be more appropriate. Deciding whether education is the most appropriate strategy for a particular problem must be one of the first decisions when planning CPD.

Hanniford suggests that

> striving for quality assurance and
> evaluating a CME programme are incompatible
> activities in some ways. The overall goal
> of a quality assurance programme, of which
> the medical audit is often a part, is the
> improvement of health care. More than one
> corrective action might be employed to
> realise that goal. If several actions are
> taken in response to identified performance
> deficiences, it is very difficult to
> determine the relative effectiveness of
> each. (Hanniford, 1981, p.27)

Nevertheless, the fact that it is difficult to quantify the precise performance outcomes of particular education programmes should not blind us to the wealth of evidence suggesting that positive overall effects on performance are associated with CPD. A recent comprehensive survey of management attitudes and training activities in British private industry and in service sectors concludes that "on every single measure high business performance is strongly and positively associated with a high level of adult training" (IFF Research Ltd for the MSC, 1985).

One important point to note is that it is not possible to evaluate the success of CPD without using some notion of what professional practice should be like. Different views of professional practice will lead to different criteria for success and different definitions of quality (Schön, 1983). The Medical Audit, for instance, seems in part to follow the medical model which sees doctors as agents and patients as the objects of (technical) professional action. Quality is then defined by evaluating the generalisable outcomes of different techniques - rather than in terms of the extent to which the unique needs of the client (the "universe of one" (Erikson, 1958, cited Schon, 1983) have been met in each case.

A similar model has been used in some evaluations of teacher performance: research which has compared the effects of particular teaching behaviours on students´ performance on standardised tests. However, Darling-Hammond et al. (1986) have noted that

> many of the (teacher) behaviours that seem
> to result in increased achievement on
> standardised tests and factual examinations
> are dissimilar, indeed nearly opposite,
> from those that seem to increase complex
> cognitive learning, problem-solving
> ability, and creativity ... Furthermore
> some research suggests that desirable
> effective outcomes of education -
> independence, curiosity and positive
> attitudes towards school, teacher and self
> - seem to result from teaching behaviours
> that are different from those prescribed
> for increasing students´ achievement on
> standardised tests of cognitive skills ...
> To confound matters further, these effects
> also seem to vary by type of student.
> (Darling-Hammond et al. 1986, p.216)

If this is the case, we cannot evaluate a teacher´s effectiveness without knowing what s/he is trying to achieve - and also knowing something about the students involved. This suggests following what has been called an "ecological" perspective (Doyle, 1978, cited Darling-Hammond et al, 1986) where researchers take into account specific contextual features such as the teacher's intentions and the way the students respond. Quality in professional practice is then seen not as a set of generalisable behaviours, but as successful adaptation to the needs of particular clients in a particular setting. However, this latter model of professional practice would lead to an entirely different way of evaluating quality, and to quite different approaches to the identification of areas for professional development from the process-product model which assumes effective behaviours are generalisable.

Donald Schön sets out these implications as follows:

> Where teachers were encouraged to reflect-in-action, the meaning of "good teaching" and "a good classroom" would become topics of urgent institutional concern. Such questions would no longer be dismissed by reference to objective measures of performance. Indeed, a major question would hinge on the relationship between such measures and the qualitative judgements of individual teachers. (Schön, 1983, p.335)

The issues we are discussing here are not specific to the two professions cited above. CPD designers for any profession need to address questions such as: What constitutes quality in practice for this group? How can it best be promoted? How should CPD be designed if it is to contribute to enhanced quality in practice? How would we know if it had done so? Another aim for this collection is to explore some of the methods and models that are available, emphasising the fact that different strategies may be appropriate in different circumstances. This strategic emphasis means that papers have been chosen not so much to represent

13

the spread of professional groupings (although a fair spread is here) but more because they exemplify different ways of tackling this common set of problems.

The papers in this book are examples of three broad strategies that CPD designers can follow. One strategy, discussed in Section One, is to address a professional group as a whole. This is the kind of brief that CPD designers are not uncommonly given. A CPD designer or provider in such a case may be employed by a professional body with the task of developing CPD for its members. Or researchers or educationalists employed within an educational institution may take on the task of identifying important educational issues for a particular professional group. The professional group in question may contain quite large numbers of practitioners and the most economical method of identifying areas for CPD will be to draw on survey research methods using results from a small sample of practitioners to provide information that can be generalised to the group as a whole. Such an approach is perhaps best suited to cases where there are good grounds for tackling features of practice that are shared by many practitioners and where the size of the professional group to be addressed makes other strategies impracticable for reasons of time and expense. It may be the only possible strategy when CPD designers are required to respond to a group in which large numbers of professionals practise independently or in small practices; or where practitioners move frequently from one employing organisation to another and cannot easily be traced.

Another strategy becomes possible, where a CPD designer relates to professionals through the auspices of an intermediary organisation: an employer, for instance, or a regional chapter of a professional body, or a group of practices that have joined together for shared CPD provision. It then becomes possible to set about devising CPD using methods that acknowledge the importance of the context for practice. For as Eraut (1982, p.11) has suggested, commenting on in-service education for teachers, "knowledge use has to be integrated with on-going institutional life" if it is to be effective.

The chapters in Section Two describe ways of designing and implementing CPD that relate to professionals within an organisational context. A key part of the CPD designer's role is then to get to know that organisation well and to work with the grain of institutional life: to understand the politics and the personalities that set the context for practice. Approaching CPD design within the framework of an organisational setting means, potentially, that CPD can be tailored more precisely to the context in which it will be implemented. What is lost in this approach is the capacity to generalise CPD needs or practice deficiencies beyond the institutional setting in which they were identified - but this loss can be offset by the important gain that support can be given to the implementation of what has been learned, and organisational barriers to implementation can be tackled alongside the CPD provision.

A third strategy, the subject of the chapters in Section Three, is to focus directly upon individual practitioners. Such a strategy is based upon a belief that personal qualities, personal experiences and personal learning styles affect the enactment of practice and therefore should be taken into account in devising a CPD agenda. More than this the focus on the individual practitioner emphasises that the most worthwhile appraisal of practice is appraisal by the person who is uniquely placed to implement recommendations arising from such an evaluation; appraisal by the person whose resistance will confound the value of the best designed programme of CPD activities.

The promotion of reflective self-evaluation is necessarily time-consuming and therefore expensive. It calls for one-to-one working between a CPD consultant and a practitioner; the resulting agenda for CPD arises from the particularities of that practitioner in relation to his/her "case-load" and has no wider application.

In emphasising self-appraisal the strategy of focusing upon individuals sets out to support practitioners in setting their own quality standards, in effect providing their own definition of what constitutes quality in practice. It is a strategy which views the professional as autonomous and leaves him or her to make the final decision about the learning needs that arise from a review of practice.

The three sections are not watertight compartments and running through them are other important themes, some of which spill over from one section to another. One important theme concerns the aim, which is shared by all these CPD designers, to narrow the gap between the practitioner and practice on the one hand - and learning on the other. In a way this demonstrates that one stage of a battle has been (largely) won. Although there will always be some laggards, to all intents and purposes all professional bodies and employers of professionals now recognise the need for professionals to take part in CPD. The acceptance of this ideal has led to the flourishing of CPD provision in recent years and this in its turn makes it possible to shift the debate on to other ground. Instead of arguing that CPD should take place we can now begin to consider what CPD should be achieving and to identify the circumstances in which it is most likely to have beneficial effects on practice.

The view that binds this collection together is that CPD should not go on separately from examinations of practice. The examination of practice can be achieved by different means: objective records of practice outcomes, simulation exercises, action research conducted by practitioners, commentaries by practice experts, collaborative corporate reviews, individual pencil and paper exercises, individual practice reviews supported by consultants or even computers, are among the examples of methods discussed in this collection. This close linking of learning to practice considerations provides the criteria on which to base plans for CPD that are more than mere forward listings. Planning CPD can then become a strategy activity in which information about practice and the practitioner may be used to set learning agendas to support future quality goals.

Although participation in CPD is on the increase there are many organisations in which no attempt is made to plan CPD. Participation often occurs in an ad hoc way without any criteria being set down as to how CPD can best contribute to a professional mission (Coopers and Lybrand Associates, 1986). Yet it seems clear that CPD stands a better chance of improving practice if it is carefully planned for the job it has to do. This collection is a contribution towards making that happen.

REFERENCES

Argyris, Chris and Schon, Donald A. (1974) Theory
in Practice.Increasing Professional
Effectiveness, Jossey-Bass, San Francisco.
Bandura, A. (1982) "Self-efficacy mechanism in
human agency", American Psychologist, 37, 2,
122-47.
Cannell, R.L. (1982) The Updating of Professional
Engineers, Centre for Extension Studies,
Loughborough University, England.
Carr-Saunders, A.M. (1928) The Professions: their
Organisation and Place in Society, Clarendon
Press, Oxford.
Cohen, Louis and Manyon, Lawrence (1980) Research
Methods in Education, Croom Helm, London.
Coles, C.R. (1977) "Developing professionalism:
staff development as an outcome of curriculum
development", Programmed Learning and
Educational Technology, 14, 4, 315-19.
Coopers and Lybrand Associates (1986) A Challenge
to Complacency: Changing Attitudes to Training.
Report to the Manpower Services Commission and
the National Economic Development Office,
Manpower Services Commission, Sheffield.
Darling-Hammond,L., Wise, A.E., and Pease,S.R.
(1986) "Teacher evaluation in the organisational
context: a review of the literature" in New
Directions in Educational Evaluation (Ernest R.
House, ed.), Falmer Press, London.
Department of Education and Science (DES) (1972)
The James Report. Teacher Education and Training,
HMSO, London.
Doyle, W. (1978) "Paradigms for research on teacher
effectiveness" in Review of Research in
Education (L.S. Schulman, ed.), Vol 5, I.E.
Peacock, Itasca, Ill.
Eraut, M. (1982) "What is learned in in-service
education and how?", British Journal of
In-Service Education, Vol 9, part 1, Autumn,
6-14.
Erikson, E. (1958) "The nature of clinical
evidence" in Evidence and Inference (Daniel
Lerner, ed.), The Free Press of Glencoe,
Glencoe, Ill.

Freidson, E. (1970) Professional Dominance, Atherton Press Inc., New York.

Gardner, R. (1978) Policy on Continuing Education: a Report with Recommendations for Action, the York Centre, University of York, York, England.

Goodlad, Sinclair (ed.) (1984) Education for the Professions, Society for Research into Higher Education and NFER-Nelson, Guildford.

Hanniford, B.E. (1981) The Medical Audit: Implications for Continuing Medical Education, Continuing Professional Education Development Project, Pennsylvania State University, Pennsylvania.

Houle, C. (1980) Continuing Learning in the Professions, Jossey-Bass, San Francisco.

IFF Research Ltd (1985) Adult Training in Britain, Manpower Services Commission, Sheffield.

Ilich, I. (1977) Disabling Professions, Marion Boyars, London.

Jarvis, P. (1983) Professional Education, Croom Helm, London.

Rogers, G.A. (1982) General Practitioners and Continuing Education: Aspects of Patient Management, M.Phil. Thesis, University of Dundee.

Schön, D.A. (1983) The Reflective Practitioner, Maurice Temple Smith, London.

Todd, F. (1985) Planning Continuing Professional Development. Planning to Improve Performance, NHS Continuing Education Unit, Institute of Advanced Architectural Studies, University of York, York.

Williams, G. (1977) Towards Lifelong Education: a New Role for Higher Education Institutions UNESCO, Paris.

Williamson, J.W., Alexander, M. and Miller, G.E. (1967) "Continuing education and patient care research", Journal of the American Medical Association, 201, 118-22.

SECTION 1:

PROFESSION-WIDE STRATEGIES

This section covers strategies of identifying continuing educational need and implementing education programmes that address professional groupings as a whole.

The profession-wide approach is usually of necessity a quantitative one, drawing on techniques from educational and social research such as representative sampling and statistical analysis for the identification of educational need.

This quantitative approach is the natural strategy to follow in circumstances where an education designer is working with large numbers of professionals from the same group and has little in the way of mediating organisations (employers, for instance) with which to work. The three papers in this section describe attempts to identify educational need respectively for five different professional groupings in the state of Pennsylvania, USA (accountants, architects, clinical dieticians, clinical psychologists and gerontic nurses); for general practitioners in the province of Limburg, the Netherlands; and for nurses in the United Kingdom. The size of the "whole" under consideration may vary (in these instances from around 400 to 400,000 practitioners) as may the definition of the "whole" (a state, a province, a country) but what these papers have in common is that they each deal with aggregated groupings of a specified profession.

When dealing with a large group it is clearly too unwieldy, too time-consuming and too costly an exercise to approach each member of the profession on an individual basis. Each of the studies in this section utilised representative sampling techniques at some point, a technique which permits findings gained from a small number of practitioners to be applied to the professional group as a whole.

Having drawn up a representative sample of practitioners, there is then the question of how to discover their continuing education needs. One strategy is simply to ask them: what they would be interested in, what relates to their work, what gives them problems. Peter Bouhuijs describes taking such perceived needs as a starting point and goes on to document the grounds for his ultimate dissatisfaction with the method - that in the end free-choice professional education does not necessarily improve professional practice.

Another strategy would be to monitor practice itself and base a curriculum around the prevention of demonstrated practice deficiencies. This is difficult to put into operation and Donna Queeney describes instead the development of simulation exercises that act as surrogates for practice. The performance of a sample of practitioners on these exercises (rated by panels of experts from the profession) is taken as indicative of what practitioner performance would be in the field. The deficiences that are found in the samples then guide the curriculum for the profession as a whole.

Yet another approach, particularly where there is little systematic information on CPD in a profession, is to try to establish what is happening currently. Using this information as a baseline, consideration can be given to deficiences not in professional practice but in existing patterns of provision and uptake of provision in that profession. This is the approach outlined by Jill Rogers in her paper. It supports recommendations about the overall design of a CPD system for nurses in the UK rather than, as in the other two cases, decisions about curriculum content in relation to the needs of practice.

Yet another way of getting a bearing upon the educational requirements of practice is to ask experienced and respected practitioners to reflect on what they see as important curriculum areas that should be addressed by CPD for their profession. In one way or another, at one stage or another, such recommendations from profession experts were used to guide CPD curriculum content for each of the groups discussed in this section. Expert professionals' recommendations may be a valuable source of guidance on commonly found practice deficiences and on what good practitioners should be able to do.

The need to address aggregates of practitioners arose in each of these cases from the starting position of the education designers and the brief agreed for them, in effect, from the type of relationship that the education designers had with the professional group. Here we see education-providing institutions taking as a unit for analysis the accountants or dieticians in the state of Pennsylvania, the GPs in Limburg province, the nurses who take up CPD in the UK. Interestingly these writers are in agreement about the need to set up some kind of local infrastructure to support the continuation of CPD (or to exploit such structures that already exist).

The methods used to identify educational need can be seen as attempting to get as close as possible to real-life practice. In just the same way the involvement of local organisations or divisions of a professional body is a way of closing the gap between the provider and the practitioner. This may be particularly important where professionals practise independently rather than within an employing organisation, or when they form a large group that is always on the move with no ready means to track practitioners from one post to another. This section includes instances of each of these possibilities.

Donna Queeney's chapter describes an innovative project which had at its heart the aim of orienting continuing professional education directly towards the needs of practice. The Continuing Professional Education Development Project, based at Pennsylvania State University and sponsored by the W.K.Kellogg Foundation, worked between 1980 and 1985 with five professions or professional specialities - accounting, architecture, clinical dietetics, clinical psychology and gerontic nursing - to develope practice-oriented educational programmes.

The Project was guided by "The Practice Audit Model", a model which had grown out of Pennsylvania State University's earlier work with the pharmacy profession, carried out in the late 1970s. The model required an initial decision that there were fruitful possibilities for collaboration between the University and a professional group, based on the satisfaction of clearly defined criteria. A substantial amount of work went into this selection process, culminating in a firm commitment to the Project from appropriate decision-makers within both the University and the professional associations.

The Practice Audit Model was then followed with these selected professions through each of its main phases. These are: organising a profession team made up of academic and professional representatives; developing a practice description, or delineation of roles carried out by practitioners within the profession; developing materials to assess practitioner performance within key roles from this listing; using these materials to run Practice Audit sessions with groups of practitioners selected to represent the whole profession; evaluating practitioner's performance on these exercises so as to establish areas of weakness; designing and planning appropriate continuing professional education programmes to improve performance in these areas; and, finally, implementing the programmes and evaluating their effectiveness. The evaluation included an assessment by participants, six months after the programme, of the extent to which they had used programme content in their practice (with reports of favourable results).

Although the Project itself has concluded, an Office of Continuing Professional Education continues Pennsylvania State University's involvement in this field and is extending and adapting the application of the Practice Audit

Model to new groups.

The strategy used in this Project to link continuing professional education to real-life practice rests upon four key elements. These are (a) the definition of practice roles, (b) the use of simulation exercises to provide an objective definition of performance standards, (c) the use of a sample of practitioners whose performance is deemed to be representative of standards in the profession as a whole, and (d) the use of self-report by practitioners participating in the programme as a means of evaluating its longer-term effects on everyday practice.

Some of these elements are also found in Chapter Two, describing Peter Bouhuijs´ work with general practitioners in the Netherlands. This is a case study of the planning and implementation of continuing medical education (CME) with a substantial proportion of the 436 registered general practitioners (GPs) in the province of Limburg.

The initial strategy in this study was to carry out a survey of GPs´ educational needs as they themselves perceived them, using a two-stage questionnaire. First 40 GPs were asked to list ten suitable topics for CME to address, then all GPs in the province were asked to assess the 68 topics on a four point scale. Here an interesting problem arose, in that analysis found an <u>inverse</u> relationship between, on the one hand, those topics that frequently occurred in a GP´s practice or those topics of general importance to GPs, and, on the other, topic areas where GPs encountered problems. The researchers found an ingenious way of utilising this anomaly to aid their design of courses.

But are the problem areas perceived by practitioners the whole story? The chapter goes on to discuss the limitations of a "perceived needs" approach, drawing particularly on two studies which found little beneficial effect on quality of practice arising from "free-choice CME". It was concluded that a better way of linking CME to quality of care would be the construction of a systematic curriculum reflecting important aspects of the work that GPs do.

The paper describes the construction of such a curriculum, themes from which were then offered to GPs in the province, each theme over a three month period, three themes per year.

A varied mix of educational formats was used to cover these themes, including course books, self-assessment materials, case studies for small group work and face-to-face events – even co-temporaneous coverage in a professional journal.

The provision of opportunities and materials for individual study and for self-help groups is an important feature of this work as is the involvement of GPs in organising the implementation of the curriculum. The need for a local system of support to service and maintain such an initiative is a clear recommendation from the study.

In Jill Rogers´ paper we move to a different order of magnitude. In 1986 there were 400,000 qualified nurses listed on the new United Kingdom professional register, with around 40,000 new admissions to the register in 1985 alone. Jill Rogers points out that the issue is not simply the size of the profession. This group is also "geographically spread and educationally diverse". When one takes into account recent changes in the profession´s structure, in the management of the National Health Service and in health care needs and trends, it becomes clear that there can be no easy answers to the question of CME provision for this large and diverse group.

The certification records for post-basic nursing qualifications showed that between 1973 and 1983 a small proportion of qualified nurses (around 10 per cent) possessed this kind of additional qualification. For a variety of reasons little was known of the use made by nurses of this involvement with CPD. Why did they undertake it, and how did it affect their careers? The study Jill Rogers describes set out to answer such questions using a questionnaire to survey a large (3,000 respondents) stratified sample of the nurses who had followed such courses. In the context of the size and geographical spread of this profession it is not surprising to find around 300 certificate courses run in course centres ranging from hospitals to colleges of education to schools of nursing. The logic behind this research was to examine the use made of these existing CPD programmes in order to move on to make coherent recommendations for the future.

To someone outside the profession one of the most striking points to emerge from this study was that almost 70 per cent of these nurses left their employing health authority to follow such a course, becoming instead temporary employees of the health authority running the course, but with no guarantee of a post after the course ended. Given that there is no increase in salary associated with these qualifications this puts rather a different complexion upon the 10 per cent participation (cited above) in these courses for the profession as a whole. The picture that emerges of these CPD participants is of a geographically mobile group committed to a particular clinical speciality and prepared to accept a degree of risk in order to improve their skills in that area - with enhanced promotion prospects quite a strong motive. It is interesting that the General Intensive Care course was seen by participants as having applications to several specialisms and was used by them as a way of rounding off basic training.

This survey is important because it shows the need for a wide-reaching system of CPD for nurses in the UK involving many more people than currently participate. Open learning systems, flexibility and a uniform system of accreditation to facilitate mobility are among Jill Rogers´ recommendations.

1 THE PRACTICE AUDIT MODEL: A NEEDS ASSESSMENT/PROGRAMME DEVELOPMENT PROCESS

Donna S. Queeney

Background

Professions by nature are complex configurations. It is easy to forget that a profession is not a single entity but a group of practitioners, each of whom is expected to subscribe to uniform standards and to practise their craft in a manner similar to that of their colleagues. Most professionals operate with a high degree of autonomy despite the influence of regulatory agencies and institutions within which they practise. Perhaps it is this lack of central control or governance that has subjected professions to increasing public criticism of the incompetence of their practitioners.

When the growth of knowledge and pace of change were relatively slow, practicing professionals were able to maintain a reasonable level of competence based on their initial pre-professional education and training. With today's knowledge explosion, however, this is no longer the case. New developments, especially within science and technology, require that highly trained professionals constantly renew their knowledge. At the same time, public accountability for professional competence has increased. As Cyril O. Houle, senior programme consultant for the W.K. Kellogg Foundation, notes, the needs of society demand improvement in professional practice, which in turn requires improved lifelong learning (Houle, 1983, p.30).

Conscientious professionals always have recognised the importance of continued learning to the maintenance of practice. They have not seen continuing professional education as a panacea or as the single means to achieving competence, but rather have viewed it as one of several tools at their disposal. However, in recent decades, as the issue of continued professional competence grew in importance, many professions began to emphasise the concept of continuing education with little attention to its true relevance to practice. The resulting expanded opportunities for continued learning that arose in the 1960s and 1970s indeed allowed "some professionals to catch up, others to keep up, and some to get ahead" (Lowenthal, 1981, p.519). Unfortunately these circumstances also resulted in a wide variety of providers offering an enormous array of courses, frequently with little thought given to either the quality of the educational experience or their relationship to improved practitioner performance.

This chapter describes a five-year research and development effort undertaken by the Pennsylvania State University to design a new approach to continuing professional education, one that would enhance its quality and its relevance to practice.

The Relationship of Continuing Professional Education in Practice

Continuing professional education, if it is to be useful, must be directly related to daily practice. In the past, decisions about the continuing education needs of practitioners frequently were based on surveys which asked respondents to identify those topics about which they would like to learn, or on faculty members´ perceptions of what practitioners should be taught. These procedures often resulted in programmes which not only failed to address practitioners´ needs, but also had little relevance to practice.

To be relevant to daily practice, continuing professional education must be tied to what practitioners actually do. This requires an understanding of the scope of practice of the profession being addressed. For example, it is not enough to determine that nurses should be taught communications skills. One must consider the specific tasks within nursing practice which require communications skills, then tailor a programme to those applications, considering such activities as building rapport with the patient, soliciting information, advising patients and families regarding care and interacting with other health care professionals.

Another point to be considered in viewing the relevance of continuing professional education to practice is that continuing professional education is designed for mid-career professionals who already have established patterns of practice. Therefore whatever knowledge and skills are taught must be integrated into existing practice patterns if they are to be applied. This situation is quite different from entry level education, in which the students have not yet developed their individual modes of professional practice.

The Continuing Professional Education Development Project, sponsored by the W.K. Kellogg Foundation and the Pennsylvania State University, was undertaken in 1980-1985 to develop new ways of designing and delivering practice-oriented continuing professional education. One of three major project goals directly addressed this issue:

> To develop and implement practice-oriented continuing professional education through the application of the Practice Audit Model to six selected professions.

The Practice Audit Model (Fig.1) is a seven-phase process intended to guide the systematic development of continuing professional education programmes that will assist practitioners in maintaining competency (Smutz et al., 1981). It provides for the identification of professional practitioners' learning needs through performance assessment and the design and delivery of programmes to address those needs. Basic to the concept of the Practice Audit Model is the notion that practice-oriented continuing professional education cannot best be accomplished by either higher educaton or the professions working alone.

The Practice Audit Model

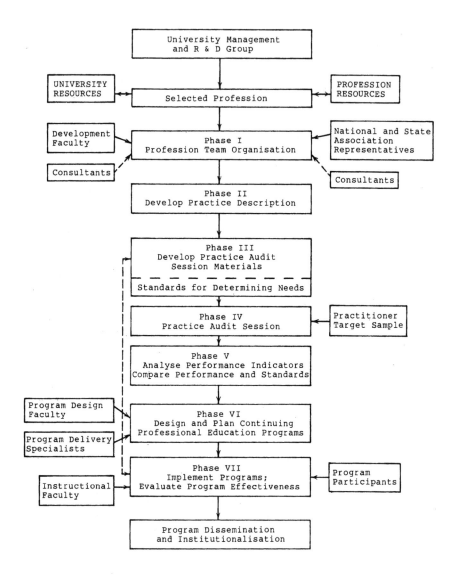

Figure 1:   Practice Audit Model

30

The Practice Audit Model

Rather, a collaborative approach which brings together the expertise of faculty members and representatives of appropriate professional associations and regulatory agencies is viewed as essential to the attainment of the above-stated goal. (Queeney, 1984; Smutz, 1984) Thus a second major project goal cited the importance of collaboration to the process:

> To establish collaborative relationships between the university and the professions in order to strengthen the development and implementation of continuing professional education programs.

As noted, the Practice Audit Model guided the work of the five-year Continuing Professional Education Development Project. However, the work of the project was seen by the Pennsylvania State University as one part of that institution's ongoing commitment to the development and delivery of continuing professional education. For this reason, a third project goal addressed the establishment of an ongoing process:

> To develop models of the university/profession collaborative relationship for continuing professional education which can lead to its institutionalisation.

The Practice Audit Model

The Practice Audit Model evolved from the Pennsylvania State University's work with the pharmacy profession. In an effort initially undertaken in 1975, four schools of pharmacy and the American Pharmaceutical Association worked with the University to define a process for determining pharmacists' practice-related needs and:

> To develop an organised, accessible, and ongoing program of continuing professional education for all pharmacist practitioners

The Practice Audit Model

which would enable them to maintain the

necessary competencies to fulfill their
role optimally. (Smutz et al., 1981, p.21)

The work of this group continued for several years.
As the group reached the point of delivering
programmes they had designed to meet identified
needs, they reviewed the steps they had taken. The
result was the Practice Audit Model, the first
application of which was to occur in the course of
the Continuing Professional Education Development
Project.

What is it that makes the Practice Audit Model
unique? First, the Model emphasises a collaborative
process, bringing together representatives of the
profession being addressed and the appropriate
academic department within a university to work in
an ongoing team which proceeds through the various
phases of the Model. In the case of the Continuing
Professional Education Development Project, the
Model was applied to five professions; for each
profession, the profession team maintained an
ongoing effort for close to five years.

Second, the Model emphasises a systematic approach
to the identification of practice-oriented needs
and the development of programmes to address those
needs. This is not a simple process, and it is a
costly one in terms of both time and money.
However, it is a thorough process, and one which
perhaps can be adapted to fit the constraints of
specific situations.

Third, the process prescribed by the Model is an
ongoing one. Far too often, continuing professional
education is a series of isolated incidents. The
iterative nature of the Model lends continuity to
the lifelong education necessary for professional
competency.

Phases of the Practice Audit Model

The Practice Audit Model consists of seven phases,

described below in terms of implementation on the Continuing Professional Education Development Project. Even prior to application of the Model, however, consideration must be given to the profession(s) to which the Model will be applied. In some cases, this will involve the selection of one or more professions with which to work. In other cases, it will require a determination regarding the appropriateness of a particular profession which wishes to apply the Model. In either circumstance, specific criteria must be considered; an attempt to apply the Practice Audit Model to a profession which is not suited to it would be both unsuccessful and frustrating. The criteria established might vary somewhat according to the specific situation. (Lindsey et al., 1986)

In the case of the Continuing Professional Education Development Project, criteria of two types were developed.

> Essential defined those criteria that the profession and the academic base must meet in order to be considered.

> Supporting defined criteria considered beneficial in that they represented an important asset, but one not required for the profession to be suitable for application of the Model. (Queeney and Melander, 1984, pp 11-12)

It should be noted that these criteria were deemed essential:

(1) an atmosphere for (university) collaboration with the professional association must exist,

(2) the profession must have addressed the issue of practice standards or developed a role delineation (a role delineation is a hierarchical description of a profession's activities organised into major domains of activity, responsibilities and tasks), and

(3) the profession must have an academic base within the Pennsylvania State University.

The Practice Audit Model

Supporting criteria were useful when a decision had to be made between two or more professions equally well qualified in terms of the essential criteria. This was important because only a limited number of professions could be selected for application of the Model through participation in the Continuing Education Development Project.

Selection of professions to participate in the Project occurred in four stages.

Identification   identity professions which meet basic requirements, thus reducing the number of professions under consideration.

Exploration   acquire detailed information about the current status and climate for continuing education within each profession still under consideration; consider the profession's academic base within the University.

Institutionalisation   consider the likelihood that the profession and the academic base would maintain the collaborative relationship following conclusion of the project.

Confirmation   meet with appropriate decision makers within the academic department and the professional associations to determine commitment to the Project.

In order for a profession to be included in the Project, agreement to participate from state and national professional associations and the academic department was essential. Perhaps surprisingly, no group which was approached declined participation. The five professions or profession specialities selected for inclusion in the Continuing Professional Education Development Project were accounting, architecture, clinical dietetics, clinical psychology and gerontic nursing. A sixth profession, medicine, was addressed by the Project but did not follow the Practice Audit Model. The Medical Audit guided the work of this profession.

Phase I: Profession Team Organisation. As noted earlier, the appropriate academic department, professional associations at the state and national levels and the national regulatory agency where appropriate came together to carry out the work of the project. Each organisation or institution appointed one or more representatives to a profession team; it was these teams that carried out the actual work of the project. Teams ranged in size from six to ten members. Each profession team met at least twice yearly, for two and a half days each time, to make key decisions and outline the work to be done. Profession team members assumed responsibility for various tasks identified in these meetings, and accomplished the necessary work between meetings.

A key factor in the smooth functioning of the profession teams was the project staff. Two project staff members were assigned to each profession team. Essentially these individuals performed the following functions:
(1) organised the activities of the profession teams to ensure that the project remained on schedule,
(2) provided background information and resources so that the teams´ decisions and actions were well grounded,
(3) established decision-making frameworks for the teams during each phase of the Practice Audit Model to keep team activities focused within the parameters of the project, and
(4) served as catalytic agents to maintain interest, enthusiasm and productivity among team members throughout the extended life of the project.

35

However, because of the collaborative nature of the project, it was essential that the project staff not be viewed as being in charge of the project. The commitment and equal participation of all team members was critical, and steps were taken to encourage these factors.

A group process consultant was hired to conduct the early meetings of all of the teams. She was viewed as a neutral person, and thus was able to minimise any perceptions of staff ownership of the project. In addition, she encouraged all team members to participate in the discussion, ensured that all viewpoints were expressed and minimised any conflicts that arose. As the teams progressed through successive meetings, it became clear that some of them no longer needed the group process consultant; team members were taking charge of their meetings and beginning to function as truly collaborative groups. As this occurred, the group process consultant withdrew from each team.

The profession teams operated by consensus. This factor was important in building members´ commitment to the project, for the team did not move ahead until all members were satisfied that the steps being taken were appropriate. Working to achieve consensus can be time consuming, and there were times when simply allowing the majority to rule was tempting; however, this was not done.

Profession team members´ participation in the Project was sponsored by the associations and institutions they represented. Their travel and living expenses incurred in attending meetings were paid for by these organisations. This arrangement not only was financially beneficial, but it also increased the organisations´ commitment to and interest in the Project.

For many of the professions, the profession team represented the first time that academic departments and professional associations had worked together in an organised, ongoing fashion. For at least one profession, the team brought together representatives of a professional association and a regulatory agency that notoriously are at odds with one another. In virtually all cases, the collaborative relationships worked exceedingly well.

Phase II: Develop Practice Description. A practice description, sometimes referred to as a role delineation, outlines the scope of practice of a given profession. Each practitioner within the profession might not do all of the things included in the practice description, but within the profession are practitioners who do all of these things. In the case of the Continuing Professional Education Development Project, a practice description was developed for each of the five professions. Each practice description was structured as described below. Generally, the practice descriptions consisted of three or four major domains, ten to fifteen responsibilities, and 70 to 120 tasks.

Level of Practice Description	Definition	Example (Based on Nursing)
Domains	broad areas of practice within the profession	provide direct patient care
Responsibilities	more specific portions of practice	assess patient condition
Tasks	specific actions or behaviours	interview patient

Developing the practice description was the first task faced by each profession team. Through discussion and using a consensual approach, domains were identified. The expertise of profession team members was an important factor in developing the drafts, and existing literature provided much of the base from which to begin. The responsibilities within each domain were listed, and the very specific tasks included in each domain were added. A draft of the practice description was outlined at the first meeting of each profession team. Staff members edited the drafts for consistency, then mailed them to profession team members for review. In the case of some professions, consensus was achieved readily; with other teams, several revisions were necessary.

In the case of architecture, a study completed in 1981 for the National Council of Architectural Registration Boards, the NCARB Examination Validation Study, provided a considerable amount of guidance. In addition, when team members had completed their practice description, it did not differ greatly from the description of practice developed in this study. Since the NCARB was based on data collected from 3,833 individuals, this close similarity was considered sufficient evidence that the practice description developed by the team reflected the realities of practice.

In the case of the other four professions, however, a survey of practitioners was conducted to determine if the practice descriptions adequately portrayed the world of practice. For each of these groups, a written questionnaire was designed, asking respondents to answer two questions for every task included in the practice description:

How important is this task to your practice?

How often do you perform this task?

Respondents were also asked to identify additional tasks not included in the practice description. The questionnaires were sent to practitioners of the profession within Pennsylvania. In all cases, the data collected indicated that the practice descriptions did indeed serve to delineate the things these practitioners did in their daily practice. In addition, the data provided a ranking of the importance and frequency with which these tasks were performed.

The Practice Audit Model

From this information and their own judgement and expertise, it was possible for the profession team to select specific responsibilities and tasks to consider further in terms of practitioners' educational needs. Obviously the initial assessment had to be limited in scope; practitioner proficiency in all responsibilities and tasks could not be assessed in the first iteration of the Practice Audit Model. Consequently, the teams chose a limited number of tasks and responsibilities on which to assess practitioners to identify areas of educational need. The selection was made on the basis of several factors:

the frequency with which survey respondents reported performing the tasks

the importance survey respondents assigned to the specific tasks

profession team members' knowledge of apparent educational need in the areas addressed by each of the responsibilities and tasks

the availability of existing programmes to improve practitioners' knowledge and skills relevant to particular responsibilities and tasks (if programmes already were available to meet educational needs, team members felt it unnecessary to develop additional programmes)

the amenability of weakness in an area of a particular responsibility or task to educational correction (for example, improvement in certain areas was more dependent upon changes in institutional policy than upon improved professional skills)

Phase III: Develop Practice Audit Session Materials
It was necessary to identify strengths and weaknesses in the areas selected for assessment; those areas in which practitioners' performance was determined to be weak would then be addressed by

39

educational programming. In order to assess practitioner performance, a Practice Audit Session was conducted for each of the five professions. This session was a day-long programme in which a sample group of practitioners participated in a variety of exercises designed to simulate practice and hence provide a measure of their performance in the practice setting.

It is important to note that the Practice Audit Sessions were intended to measure the performance of the group of practitioners studied rather than individual performance. The practitioners selected to participate in each each Practice Audit Session were considered representative of their colleagues. Thus group scores on the exercises were defined, and areas of educational need were identified on the basis of the group performance.

The Practice Audit Sessions were designed following assessment centre methods. These methods require specific exercises be developed to put the individual being tested in a simulated practice situation, so that his or her professional skills can be measured. Many different types of exercises may be used: role playing, live simulations, in-basket techniques, case studies, trigger films, paper and pencil exercises, etc. The intent is to create a situation as close to actual practice as possible.

The task facing the profession teams was twofold: team members had to develop exercises that would measure practitioners' performance in the specific areas selected for study, and they had to develop valid, reliable methods of measuring that performance against criteria they established. Because these activities required considerable expertise in testing and measurement, a consultant was hired to work with team members at their meetings and as they designed the exercises and evaluation criteria. Standards of acceptable performance also had to be established; at what point was a practitioner's performance deemed acceptable, and at what point was it considered weak?

Each Practice Audit Session included quite a range of exercises. Many of them had at least one live simulation in which an actor portrayed a patient or client with whom each participant was required to interact. In these live simulations, the participant was given written material describing the background of the case, a specific assignment for working with the client or patient and then asked to meet with the individual for a specified length of time. For example, clinical dieticians were asked to talk with a "diabetic patient" (portrayed by an actress) and to teach her about proper diet for her condition. Accountants met with the "president" of a business to discuss his tax returns. These live simulations were videotaped and later evaluated by trained raters, using evaluation criteria developed by profession team members.

Another form of exercise was a trigger film; participants were shown a film portraying, for example, a nurse working with a dying patient. The film was stopped at specific intervals, and participants were asked questions regarding the way in which the nurse handled the situation and the steps they would take in that situation. Also, case studies, in which participants were asked to prepare a patient care plan or an accounting report, were used. The entire Architecture Practice Audit Session was based upon one case study which presented the problem of designing a town hall for a fictitious community.

Phase IV: The Practice Audit Session. Even as the exercises described above were being developed, plans were being made for the Practice Audit Sessions. Identification of individuals to participate in the sessions was critical. In most cases, Pennsylvania practitioners were invited to the sessions, and participants were chosen from among those who responded. In one case, gerontic nursing, employers were asked to nominate "typical" staff nurses caring for older adults, and participants were chosen from the pool of those nominated. An effort was made to obtain a sample of practitioners that was representative of the profession. Respondents were paid for their travel to and from the Practice Audit Sessions, their meals while there, and their lodging as appropriate. However, they did not receive any honorarium or wages for participation in the sessions.

Each Practice Audit Session was a full day in length, although the formats of the sessions varied. Some of them began early in the morning and ended by late afternoon. Others began immediately following lunch on one day and concluded at noon the next day, allowing participants time to travel to and from the site immediately prior to and following the session. The schedule for each session was carefully co-ordinated and was quite tight; there was no wasted time. However, breaks were built into the schedule, and care was taken to ensure a pleasant experience for all participants.

In all cases, participants were divided into small groups at the start of the Practice Audit Session. Each group was led by a member of the profession team. Although the exercises were completed by each individual working alone, the groups gave participants an opportunity for peer interaction between activities, and reduced the likelihood of participants feeling threatened by the assessment experience.

Interestingly enough, participants in the Practice Audit Sessions viewed them as a learning experience, although they were of course intended to test rather than to teach. The utilisation of small groups was felt to be particularly useful because of the opportunity for exchange of ideas that the groups provided. From these participant observations, profession team members gained some insights into methods that might be applied to the delivery of the educational programmes they were about to develop.

Phase V: Analyse Performance Indicators, Compare Performance and Standards. Once the Practice Audit Sessions had been completed, it was necessary to evaluate participants' performance on each exercise. Rating scales, scoring sheets and other appropriate devices had been developed and were applied. Profession team members reviewed the results of each exercise, considering how the group of participants performed. From these data, and using the performance standards established by the profession team, it was possible to identify those areas in which the participants did well, and those in which they exhibited some weakness. On the basis of this information, specific areas were selected for educational programming.

Phase VI: Design and Plan Continuing Professional Education Programme. As the profession teams approached the development of educational programmes, they gave considerable thought to the selection of appropriate methods for teaching and delivering the programmes. Some of the deficiencies uncovered in the Practice Audit Sessions, as well as participants' responses to the sessions themselves, indicated that the teaching of needed skills could best be accomplished by providing practitioners with an opportunity to practise those skills after learning about them. For example, accountants, who demonstrated some difficulty interacting with clients, needed to be taught communications skills. However, a lecture or even a demonstration of these skills would not be sufficient to ensure that the practitioner could learn those skills and implement them satisfactorily; a next step, that of practising the skill in the learning environment where feedback was available, was necessary if the programme truly was to allow participants to relate their learning to practice. Because this was true of many of the skills in which practitioners in all the professions studied were deficient, a number of the programmes were designed to include skills practice and application as an integral part of the educational experience.

The profession teams developed the concepts for the programmes to be offered. As they found that additional expertise in instructional design, available media for delivery and marketing were needed, they called upon consultants to work with them to turn their ideas into viable programmes. Personnel from the Pennsylvania State University's Divisions of Continuing Education and of Media and Learning Resources provided necessary assistance in

43

the areas of media application and programme delivery, while faculty members were able to help with programme design and content. Professional association members also were called upon as appropriate.

For several of the professions, at least some of the areas of weakness that were identified were not based in the academic discipline of the profession. In the example cited above, for example, accountants´ need for communication skills required expertise from the Department of Speech Communication. However, because a faculty member from this area was not likely to have a thorough understanding of the accounting profession, it was deemed advisable to have the instruction designed and provided by a combination of faculty members and practitioners representing both disciplines. In all cases, profession team members were not hesitant to identify individuals with greatest expertise in the areas to be addressed, whether within the university, the professional association, or the profession at large.

Several of the programmes required the development of written materials, videotapes or other educational materials. Again, profession team members worked with the project staff and appropriate service units within the University to produce these materials.

Phase VII: Implement Programmes; Evaluate Programme Effectiveness. Programmes were planned for delivery at a variety of locations across Pennsylvania. In consultation with The Pennstlvania State University´s Continuing Education delivery system, profession team and project staff members decided upon appropriate locations, dates, and scheduling formats. Seven programmes were offered during the course of the Continuing Professional Education Development Project, and continue to be delivered to new audiences.

Participants in each programme have been asked to evaluate the programme upon its completion. In this manner, suggestions for subsequent offerings of the programmes are obtained. These evaluations have ranged from good to excellent, indicating that professionals find the programmes relevant to their practice, as well as interesting and well-presented.

Because of the strong emphasis on practice orientation, a follow-up evaluation has been conducted for a number of the programmes. Participants have been sent a questionnaire approximately six months after the programme asking them how they have used the information presented in the programme. These evaluations too have been quite favourable; participants report that the programmes have indeed had an effect on their patterns of practice.

Programme Dissemination and Institutionalisation

The offical conclusion of the Continuing Professional Education Development Project in no way marked the conclusion of these activities. Rather, the Pennsylvania State University and the participating professional associations and regulatory agencies view the work of the five-year project as an important base on which to build. Activities and initiatives emanating from the Project take several forms.

Programme Dissemination. The programmes developed in the course of the project were viewed, in their first delivery, as pilot programmes. On the basis of participation and profession team members' evaluations, those programmes have been modified as appropriate and are being offered to other audiences, and sometimes in other formats or through other delivery media. An architecture programme on cost control, initially delivered as a seminar, has been prepared for delivery as an independent study course. A programme for dieticians has been divided into segments, with the resultant smaller programmes being offered in conjunction with professional meetings. Programmes developed for nurses are being recast into modules for on-site delivery in both acute care and extended care facilities.

As the dissemination of these programmes continues,

the responsibilities of the university and the professional associations require some specification. Because each profession is organised differently, and each professional association is unique, these relationships are being arranged on an individual basis. In the case of accounting, for example, the Pennsylvania Institute of Certified Public Accountants has assumed responsibility for marketing and delivery of programmes, while the Pennsylvania State University provides the educational materials necessary each time the programme is offered.

While the programmes initially were offered within Pennsylvania, they now are being made available throughout the United States.

Institutionalisation. As noted earlier, the institutionalisation of ongoing collaborative relationships for the development and delivery of continuing professional education programmes has been an integral part of the effort described here. Organisations enter into new relationships slowly and cautiously, and changes within an organisation are slow to occur. Therefore institutionalisation is a lengthy process. However, it is the belief of those engaged in the Continuing Professional Education Development Project that progress has been made in this area, in both the university and the professional associations engaged in the project.

Within the Pennsylvania State University, the Office of Continuing Professional Education was established in August 1985 to carry on the work begun by the five-year endeavour. An indication of the university's commitment to continuing professional education, the Office has several aspects to its mission.

To continue to work with academic departments, professional associations and regulatory agencies to develop and deliver practice-oriented continuing professional education programmes. In this role, the

Office functions as a catalyst, bringing together the resources necessary, from both within and outside of the university. Delivery of existing programmes will be expanded, as described above, and new programmes will be developed and prepared for delivery.

To promote and encourage participation in continuing professional education activities within the university, by serving as consultant to faculty members and others as they initiate and expand their work in this area.

To adapt and apply the Practice Audit Model, and portions thereof. Particular emphasis will be on the area of needs assessment, in the belief that the identification of practice-related educational needs is crucial to the development of meaningful continuing professional education.

To develop continuing professional education curricula in a movement toward the formation of lifelong learning patterns. Continuing professional education, which has been episodic in the past, must be provided in a consistent, coherent pattern if it is to contribute to the maintenance of professional competency.

To explore the development of learning support systems, so that practitioners may have the necessary encouragement and reinforcement to apply their newly gained skills over time.

To conduct research in continuing professional education.

Conclusion

The Practice Audit Model, developed at the

The Practice Audit Model

Pennsylvania State University in the late 1970s and applied there through the Continuing Professional Education Development Project 1980-1985, offers a unique approach to the assessment of professional practitioners' educational needs and the development of practice-oriented educational programmes to address those needs. It has been proven successful in many respects, yet it is not without its problems.

First, practice-oriented continuing professional education, by its very nature, is costly to develop and deliver. Identification of needs and presentation of programmes which offer participants an opportunity to practise that which is taught require large expenditures of both time and money. This outlay in turn dictates that the programmes themselves are expensive, so that participation may be somewhat limited. This problem must be addressed by answering several questions:

(1) Who should pay for continuing professional education? Is it the participant, the employer, the profession or some combination?
(2) Are there ways of reducing the costs of such programmes through economies of scale, improved exploitation of available media or otherwise?
(3) Can the high costs of programmes designed to teach skills be offset by other, less costly programmes?

Second, the very thorough type of needs assessment included in the Continuing Professional Education Development Project may be beyond the reach of some professions in terms of the resources and expertise required; it can be unwieldy. It should be considered one way of identifying learning needs, but other viable means of needs assessment must be developed.

Third, continuing professional education is not yet in the mainstream, or the core, of higher education in the United States. Preoccupations with research and publication, requisites for promotion and tenure on campuses across the country, tend to take priority over even traditional teaching at many institutions. Needed is the recognition that colleges and universities, as centres of learning, are responsible not only for preparation of the entry level professional, but also for helping that professional to maintain competency throughout his or her career. This recognition must come from higher education institutions' central administrations and from the faculty, and it must be addressed in the policies governing higher education institutions.

Fourth, the professional associations, and to a lesser extent the regulatory agencies, vary widely in their perspectives on continuing professional education. For some it is seen as a means of policing practitioners' competency, for others it is perceived primarily as a source of revenue, regardless of the reasons for its growth. These organisations and the practitioners they represent must come to see continuing learning as an essential component of professional practice, one that should be made as meaningful, and hence useful, as possible.

On the brighter side, many positive notions emerged from this project. The practice-oriented continuing professional education programmes developed indeed have appeared to have a very real influence on participants' practice. The process through which they were developed, although complex, has been proven workable and does lend itself to streamlining, which will increase its applicability.

Perhaps the most substantial success of the project was the establishment and maintenance of collaborative working relationships. The benefits of higher education/professional association collaboration, long suspected, have been shown to be substantial. Collaboration is not easily achieved: collaborating parties must be carefully chosen, have compatible (but not conflicting) goals and each possess resources from which the other(s) can benefit. However, in the area of continuing professional education, the gains to be realised through collaboration certainly justify the effort.

The field of continuing professional education is,

The Practice Audit Model

in the 1980s, in its infancy. Through thoughtful
and thorough research and development efforts such
as the Continuing Professional Education
Development Project, it will grow in both stature
and scope.

REFERENCES

Houle, Cyril O. (1980) <u>Continuing Learning in the Professions</u>, Jossey-Bass, San Francisco, California, USA.

Lindsay, Carl A.,Crow, Mary Deth & Jacobs, Durand, F. (1986) "Continuing professional education for clinical psychology: a practice-oriented model" in <u>Evaluation and Accountability in Clinical Training</u> (Barry Edelstein and Ellen Berler, eds.), Plenum Press, New York, USA.

Lowenthal, Werner (1981) "Continuing education for professionals - voluntary or mandatory?" , <u>Journal of Higher Education</u>, Vol 52 (5) 519-535.

National Council of Architectural Registration Boards (1981) <u>NCARB Examination Validation Study</u>, National Council of Architectural Registration Boards, Washington, D.C. USA

Queeney, Donna S. (1984) "The role of the university in continuing professional education", <u>Educational Record</u>, 65:3, Summer, 13-17

Queeney, Donna S. and Melander, Jacqueline J. (1984) <u>The Profession Selection Process</u>, The Pennsylvania State University, University Park, Pennsylvania, USA.

Smutz, Wayne D. <u>Formal Boundary Spanners and Organizational Change: Establishing University/Professional Association Interorganization Relationships</u> Unpublished Ph.D. dissertation, The Pennsylvania State University.

Smutz, Wayne D., Kalman, S.H., Lindsay, C.A., Pietrusko, R.G. and Seaman, J.J. (1981) <u>The Practice Audit Model: A Process for Continuing Professional Education Needs Assessment and Program Development</u>, The Pennsylvania State University, University Park, Pennsylvania, USA

2 PLANNING CONTINUING MEDICAL EDUCATION FOR GENERAL PRACTITIONERS IN THE NETHERLANDS (1)

Peter A.J.Bouhuijs

Introduction

This chapter deals with important issues in planning continuing education programmes. Since learning by practice is a very effective way of learning, a case study is presented here which describes the planning and implementation of a continuing medical education (CME) programme for general practitioners (G.P.s) in the province of Limburg, the Netherlands. The chapter starts with some background information on CME for general practitioners. Some general planning approaches for CME are described next. This is followed by a study of perceived needs of G.P.s which was carried out in Limburg. The limitations of this approach are dealt with in the next section. A system curriculum approach which complements the perceived needs approach is then described, including the first outcomes of this approach. The concluding sections deal with the future of this approach in Limburg and the possible lessons for other fields of continuing education.

CME for G.P.s: Some Background Information

Continuing medical education for general practitioners is a steadily growing field of professional education in most European countries. Although there is an increasing public pressure in Europe to introduce legal obligations to participate in CME courses, only two countries, West Germany and Italy, have actually taken initiating measures. Others, i.e. England, Norway and Belgium, have put a premium on attendance at a minimum number of CME courses.

Planning Continuing Medical Education

The profession itself, generally, is opposed to compulsory arrangements. A report by the European Union of General Practitioners (UEMO) says:

> Although continuing education is a moral obligation on every doctor and legal provisions to support and encourage participation in continuing education may be of value, UEMO is opposed to any legal obligation to take part with some sort of sanction for those who do not fulfil such a requirement. (UEMO, 1979)

In the Netherlands there are neither legal obligations nor rewards.

In most countries both the profession and universities have taken an interest in organising CME courses. In the Netherlands the generally scattered activities of the profession have been co-ordinated since 1973 by a foundation, which activates regional G.P. activities, provides support, both financial and professional, for course production and plays an active role in the discussion about the future of CME. CME organisation structures have changed in pursuance of the new legislation introduced in 1977. The whole field of continuing education for all academic areas is now regulated by a special Act. National committees, in which the profession and all relevant faculties are represented, are made responsible for the general planning of CME in a particular field. Regional committees, in which one faculty and professionals from the region concerned have a seat can be set up to co-ordinate CME on the regional level. Universities are responsible for implementing the courses initiated by regional or national committees.

The organisation of CME courses for general practitioners in the Dutch province of Limburg is presented in this chapter as a case study to show the evolution of planning concepts through the interaction between a medical faculty and general practitioners, supported by field studies concerned with CME planning.

Planning Continuing Medical Education

Limburg, the southernmost province of the Netherlands, lies in an isolated position from a national point of view. In medicine, co-operation across European borders is very limited. Until the start of a new medical faculty in the province in 1974, an important feature of which is its dedication towards primary care, local general practitioners organised their own programmes for continuing education. An enthusiastic group of G.P.s representing the subregions of the province started in 1968 with the support of a pharmaceutical industry (Merck, Sharpe and Dohme). The involvement of the faculty of medicine was initially restricted to an educational adviser for course planning and evaluation. Gradually this regional initiative has evolved to its current position as official regional planning committee for CME, in which faculty and G.P.s share responsibilities.

General Principles of CME

Theoretically CME planning is an easy matter: CME is to be designed to eliminate existing deficiences in health care delivery and is also to include new developments in medicine and health care. The first part is the hardest to realise in a practical situation. Generally, four approaches are available to assess the need for CME (Bouhuijs, 1981):

(1) quality assessment of health services;

(2) survey of perceived needs of G.P.s;

(3) survey of perceived needs of other health professionals (specialists);

(4) survey of perceived needs of consumers of health services.

Laxdal (1982) states that both perceived (subjective) needs and real (objective) needs are to be taken into account. In a practical sense, however, quality assessment of health services has not much to offer to course planners at the moment.

Planning Continuing Medical Education

Lack of standard procedures, lack of standardised records, high cost of quality of care research and reluctance on the part of professionals to be monitored are some of the problems with which this important field of research is confronted.

For a CME planning committee the second option, perceived needs of G.P.s, is the most feasible. Initially, the committee itself chose the topics of CME courses, mainly using their own experience as G.P.s as a criterion. Gradually, it came to be felt that this was not a satisfactory planning basis. For one of the annual courses, "New Developments in Medicine", regional specialists were invited to suggest topics for inclusion. Also, during some CME courses, participants were invited to list topics for future courses. In 1980 the committee decided that a systematic survey of perceived needs among all G.P.s in the province should be carried out in order to set up long-term CME planning.

Survey of Perceived Needs

A French G.P., Leoni(1979), described a two step method to identify continuing education needs of general practitioners. A group of practitioners is asked to draft a list of possible topics (the first step); after some arrangements to exclude overlapping suggestions the group then rates each suggestion on five aspects:

(1) frequency of occurrence in the practice;
(2) general importance of the topic to G.P.s;
(3) problems encountered by G.P.s in the area of:

    (a) knowledge;
    (b) practical skills;
    (c) attitude towards the patient.

The method is described as a tool to be used in meetings of G.P.s to reach consensus on course planning. For our purpose we modified this idea into a two step questionnaire, which could be used for large groups. The first part of the project involved the composition of a list of topics, which was to be assessed by all G.P.s in the province in the second part of the study.

In the first part of the study forty G.P.s were asked to mention ten subjects of possible interest for a CME course. The group consisted of 10 CME committee members, 10 staff members of the university department of General Practice and 20 randomly selected G.P.s from the region. Seventy-five per cent of the sample responded and suggested an averaged number of six topics per person. The resulting 170 suggestions were compiled into a list of 68 subjects by combining overlapping or similar topics.

In the second part of the study these 68 topics had to be assessed by all G.P.s in the province on the five aspects mentioned before, on a four-point scale. A number of topics of a general nature, such as "how to anticipate in health care" or "evaluating work procedures" could not be included in the questionnaire.

All registered G.P.s of the province, 408 persons in total, were sent this questionnaire, which is partly reproduced in Figure 1. Given the content of the questionnaire anonymity of the respondents was guaranteed. In order to be able to do some control studies on the data and to send a reminder to non-respondents, a business reply card was included on which G.P.s could indicate whether or not they had sent in the questionnaire. Reminders were then sent to all who failed to send in this card. Sixty-four per cent participated in the study, which is an acceptable proportion for a mailed questionnaire. There were no differences between respondents and non-respondents in participation in three CME courses, organised in the previous year.

	frequency per year	importance for G.P.	problems you face in the areas of		
			knowledge	skills	attitudes
1 =	seldom	unimportant	no problems		
2 =	sometimes	some importance	some problems		
3 =	often	important	problems		
4 =	very often	very important	major problems		
1. prescriptions for dermatological problems					
2. emergency first aid					
3. treatment of pain					

Figure 1: Format of the perceived needs survey (partly reproduced) for a CME course

A first analysis of the results indicated that the suggested scoring method of Leoni, i.e. counting the scores of the five criteria, was not the best way to find the topic of greatest relevancy. Frequency and importance on the one hand and problem scores on the other proved to be inversely related ($r = -0.52$). Simple addition would result in scores in a limited range and be hard to interpret in terms of CME priorities. We therefore introduced an alternative scoring method by which all subjects could be split up in a 2x2 table (see Figure 2), treating frequency and importance as one dimension and problems encountered as another.

High frequency/importance score   Low frequency/importance score

	High frequency/importance score	Low frequency/importance score
High problem score	backpain chronic complaints identification of relational problems somatic fixation indications for physiotherapy headache depression early diagnostics and treatment for cancer how to deal with anxiety and tension nutrition patterns and disorders dizziness drug-interactions of common prescriptions patient education revalidation after infarction	psychotherapy in general practice * foreign workers' problems drug addiction electrocardiography for GPs ** interpretation of modern X-ray and isotope techniques funduscopy chronic fatigue genetic counselling GP and social security regulations neurological screening of young children psychology of the elderly protoscopy ** self-help groups paracentesis varices infusion chronic glaucoma ** homosexuality in adolescents ** audiometry
Low problem score	prescriptions for dermatological problems pain in the neck, shoulders and arms care for chronical patients psycho-pharmaceuticals diagnostics for geriatric problems prescriptions and geriatric problems percussion and auscultation treatment of pain GP-specialist communication selective use of lab data CARA sport traumata first aid foot problems rheumatism death and dying allergology contraception slimming-courses intestinal problems nose and sinuses wound treatment eye infections menopause problems decompensation removal of corpora alieni from the eye minor surgery	recognising and preventing communicable diseases * revalidation of CVA varicose ulcer mouth and chew problems ** implanting I.U.D's liver disorders epilepsy obstetrics for GPs hyperthyroidism

* indicates a higher problem score for young physicians

** indicates a higher score for experienced physicians

Figure 2: Sixty-eight topics for CME courses arranged for frequency/importance score and problem score, based on 260 G.Ps´ preferences.

Planning Continuing Medical Education

In terms of course planning, different course formats can be used for different categories. Topics that have a high problem score call for an interaction format, in which participants can formulate their problems and acquire the skills necessary to overcome them. High frequency/importance scores are a kind of popularity index and can be used as an indication for the number of participants when a course is organised.

Since respondents were asked to indicate how many years they had practised, it was possible to look for differences between subgroups. Generally no major differences in preference were found. In Figure 2 the topics for which younger practitioners (3-5 years in practice) or experienced practitioners (over 15 years in practice) had a higher problem score than the total group of respondents are marked with asterisks.

The outcomes of the study proved to be a useful tool for planning several courses which attracted reasonable numbers of general practitioners.

Limitations of a Perceived Needs Approach

As a marketing tool the method worked quite well, but the limitations of the approach rapidly became clear as well. A nice illustration was provided by the remarks of a neurologist on the low scores for epilepsy. He mentioned that one of the basic problems for a G.P. is to recognise the signs and symptoms of the disease in an early stage. As long as the people concerned do not understand that there is a problem, one can hardly expect that perceived needs will show the importance of this problem. For a limited group of G.P.s a course was organised on this topic after which participants acknowledged their blind spots in this area. This illustrates a general problem of general practice as a profession, which is the relative isolation of general practitioners in their work: not only do they work as solo practitioners to a large degree, but regular feedback on the quality of their work is generally lacking. Patients provide limited feedback, consulting specialists are reluctant to be very critical since their stream of patients (and income) is dependent upon the G.P., and medical audit is not in good shape yet in general practice. As a consequence one can expect blind spots in the needs perception of G.P.s.

Two studies influenced the development of an alternative CME planning approach in Limburg. The first study is the much cited Sibley et al.(1982) study on the effects of CME. In an elegant design the investigators evaluated the long-term effects on the quality of care of free-choice and assigned CME packages. It turned out that free-choice CME did not have any effect on quality of care parameters when compared to a control group not attending CME. G.P.s who studied an assigned CME package did significantly better than a control group. This outcome underscores the limitations of a planning approach depending on the perceived needs of G.P.s.

The second study was an evaluation study on the long-term learning effects of one-week CME courses in Limburg. Metsemakers, Bouhuijs and Beusmans (1983) used a self-report method combined with follow-up structured interviews to investigate the effects of such a course. The main reason for this approach was the problem-based format: during one week a group of about 15 G.P.s discussed prepared cases and could apply to specialist consultants for information and feedback. This CME model, called the Warffum model, is a popular format in the Netherlands. The evaluation of the learning effects is not a simple one, due to the open character of the course: participants themselves determine to a large degree the range of learning effects, so that a standard test is not a good method to search for those effects. Using the paradigm of "illuminative evaluation", (Parlett and Dearden, 1977), the investigators tried to tap the effects from a learner's point of view. All 33 participants of two Warffum courses were asked to report on what they had gained (further referred to as learning points) after each half-day session.

The second focus of this study was to look for

long-term effects of those learning points in practice. After six months, all participants were interviewed by a G.P. investigator about their learning points. It turned out that more than 40% of the learning points were seen as important because they were considered a reassurance with regard to their established way of practising in that area.

Over 50% of the learning points related to intended changes in procedures. The remainder represented those areas in which G.P.s noted differences of opinion, without an intention to change their viewpoint. The relevant outcome of this study is the high percentage of learning points which reflect reassurance of procedures already established in practice.

These findings suggest that attending a CME course not only reflects a thirst to learn something new, but also a need to be reinforced in common work procedures, which is a factor not included in the earlier mentioned perceived needs study.

The results of studies of this kind imply that problem areas perceived by G.P.s represent only a part of their needs.

Description and Rationale of a Curriculum Approach

Both studies cited here suggest for various reasons that CME planning based on G.P. perceived needs, tapped by an inventory, is not the best option for a quality of care assessment approach. Our conclusion from these studies is that a systematic curriculum containing key topics for G.P.s is a better way to ensure the effectiveness of CME.

In September 1983 the regional planning committee adopted this idea of a systematic curriculum. In fact, this decision marked a considerable shift in the planning approach, which can be characterised as a norm-oriented approach which complements the marketing approach.

Based on two recent reports about tasks and

functions of general practitioners (Van Es, 1983; Landelijke Huisartsen Vereniging, 1982), a preliminary list of topics was made representing the common aspects of a general practitioner´s work. It was felt that a CME curriculum reflecting systematically the important aspects of a G.P.´s task could also enable G.P.s to get a better overview of the current requirements of their profession.

The curriculum focuses systematically on important aspects of a G.P.´s task. Each year three themes are offered for three months each. For each theme a loose-leaf coursebook is prepared which contains an overview of important topics related to the theme, self-assessment materials, treatment protocols, case studies for small group work, review articles, suggested further readings and announcements of a variety of course activities. Each coursebook marks the start of a three months´ period in which several events are offered: short two hour meetings in subregions, a one day regional course, opportunities to test knowlege and skills and opportunities to ask for more information . An annual one week residential course in a small group setting provides additional learning opportunities in the three themes of that year. An overview of one of the themes is presented in Figure 3.

The mixture of self-learning materials and varied course formats is chosen for several reasons. A deliberate attempt has been made to combine the features of an independent learning system with a social support system. Dunn and Hamilton (1985) summarise criteria for distance learning provisions for continuing professional education.

1. Coursebook "The cancer patient".
   This book is distributed free of charge to all
   general practitioners in the region.
   Contents:
   - objectives for CME
   - epidemiological information on tumors
   - self-test (true/false format)
   - overview of available courses and seminars
   - paper patient simulations using the modified
     essay format; for home use of small group
     meetings
   - selected references (literature and
     audiovisuals)
   - business reply cards to order literature,
     audiovisuals, additional test, information on
     ICI drugs.

2. One day course "The cancer patient".
   Large group lectures; same programme is offered
   in two towns on consecutive days.
   - simulated patient work up, followed by small
   group discussions
   - short lectures by specialists, followed by
     discussion
   - skills training session
   - application of decision theory.

3. One day course "Progress in medicine"
   Large group lectures; same programme is offered
   in two towns on consecutive days.
   Part of the programme on cancer related topics.

4. Three and a half day residential course.
   Annual course using a problem solving, small
   group approach. One day of the course is spent
   on cancer problems, including home care, breast
   cancer, pitfalls in cancer treatment,
   counselling cancer patients.

5. Subregional short courses.
   Two hour short courses offered in four different
   towns. Organisers can choose from eight
   different prepared courses.

6. Special issue of "The Practitioner" on cancer
   problems.
   This journal issue contains some of the lecture
   materials from the courses and selected
   contributions from the British version of "The
   Practitioner".

Figure   3: Overview course programme on "the cancer patient"

1. The provision must be convenient for professionals to use in practice.

2. Educational materials should be competitively packaged and presented.

3. Information given to professionals must always be concise.

4. Materials should be based on competencies needed, in other words, be relevant.

5. The provision has to be flexible to allow adaptation to individual needs.

6. Self-assessment is an essential element of any provision.

7. Successful continuing education must also include areas of speculation – the so-called grey areas of professional practice where different courses of action might be successful for different people.

8. Continuing education must be systematic in its coverage.

Most of these points are incorporated in the curriculum approach. From an educational point of view it is also important to provide a social structure in which independent learning can take place. Neil (1981) concludes from experiences in seventeen countries with distance learning systems (such as Open Universities) that groups of students coming together to learn significantly increase learning and/or decrease drop-out. Therefore courses are included in the curriculum as a necessary complement of self-study materials.

The variety of learning is also important in view of differences between participants in entrance levels, learning styles and preferences for learning activities (Curry,1983). There are also more practical reasons: practice patterns differ in many ways; this can influence the preference for short courses of some practitioners and for one week courses of others. Financial aspects and the level of co-operation between practitioners in a certain area can also play a role.

In each coursebook a specification of the topics is presented based on epidemiological data in the Netherlands. A team of planners, representing various disciplines, then prepares the actual courses and learning materials.

The curriculum is co-ordinated by the regional committee for continuing medical education, in which the faculty of medicine and the representatives of general practitioners have an equal number of seats. In the planning of the programme already existing structures are used, such as local planning committees and a planning team for the residential course. Financial support for the implementation comes from various sources: the administrative centre is supported by a government grant and by the university; the faculty of medicine supports the programme further by teaching manpower; the general practitioners pay fees for some courses and also participate in the planning; a successful attempt has been made to attract sponsors for the courses. Three major industries (ICI, Glaxo, and Beecham) supported the curriculum in its first year. The regional cancer institute supported the cancer course. An agreement was also made with a CME journal (The Practitioner) to synchronise themes in the journal with the programme, and to publish some of the course materials.

Evaluation

The evaluation of this programme offers a number of problems: since the approach is new, it is hard to predict what level of participation can be expected; it is also difficult to evaluate the home use of the materials; and evaluation of CME is generally a harder job than evaluating a course in a medical school.

Planning Continuing Medical Education

In this report we confine ourselves to the 436 registered G.P.s in the province of Limburg. Most of the activities organised also attracted other interested health professionals, such as G.P. trainees, G.P.s from other parts of the country, faculty staff, and other specialists.

During this first year the participation of general practitioners was analysed from available information at the CME office; since a number of local activities are not included, the participation rates represent a conservative estimate. Twenty general practitioners were randomly chosen to be interviewed by telephone in order to collect information on the perception of the programme by general practitioners. Results of the data analysis were discussed by a panel of six general practitioners, representing local CME committees.

Participation

Out of a total of 436 registered general practitioners in the region 210 participated at least once in the activities offered in the curriculum during the year. Since a number of local courses were not included in the analysis, it seems fair to conclude that 50% of the general practitioners participated in at least one activity in the curriculum. 10% of the practitioners participated in the annual residential course.

From the interviews it can be concluded that it is unlikely that there will be a substantial additional number of general practitioners who do not show up at meetings, but who use the materials otherwise.

Although a 50% participation rate seems a reasonable result, a breakdown by courses showed that the first theme attracted quite a high number of participants, but that the number dropped significantly in later courses.

From the interviews and the panel results one can

get some important clues to explain these results. There was certainly an element of "newness" in the first course. The curriculum was introduced in two special sessions at the university which attracted over 200 general practitioners. A number of practitioners expressed their disappointment afterwards with the one day course, which resembled very much the approach that was used in earlier courses. Apparently the relation between organised activities and self study materials was not very clear.

In general "disappointments" seem to have a multiplier effect: when you did not like it the first time, you do not return for a second try.

Some general practitioners complained about the complexity of the course book. Although the course planners stress the menu approach, participants feel overwhelmed by the options offered, which turns them off.

About half of the interviewed practitioners said they had tried the self tests, but only a few claimed to use the tests regularly; case studies were seldom used individually, but at least four groups (about 40 G.P.s) used those materials in their monthly local meetings. About 80% of the interviewed G.P.s supported the idea of a longitudinal thematic approach.

Another explanation is the less active role of the general practitioner organisation in the implementation of the curriculum. Although the continuous input of the practitioners was generally seen as an important factor for the success of the approach, too little attention has been given to the grassroot level in CME.

Some Conclusions for the Future
It is clear that an essential goal of this approach, namely to convince G.P.s that using the curriculum approach is a good way to keep up with your profession, has not been reached yet: in spite of its official status the materials and courses are not generally seen as the most important

source. Given the critique on the first year, some attention should be given to prove the assumed quality of this approach.

It is clear that a good balance between organised activities and self study has not been reached in the first year of operation. The curriculum approach as such has attracted considerable attention: sponsors, providers and potential customers agree that a really continuous approach is an essential step to achieve the general goals of professional development. More attention needs to be given to measures which support the local use of CME materials. Several approaches are available here: CME faculty can help local groups in using the materials by offering help in conducting meetings or providing feedback; local hospitals (generally not yet involved in the curriculum) could synchronise their programmes with the thematic approach; the complexity of the materials could be reduced by a clearer modular approach; since local success seems to be related to active individuals, it seems important to support local leadership.

Conclusions for Other Disciplines

From the case study presented here some conclusions can be drawn which are not restricted to continuing education for general practitioners, but which are also relevant for other professions. Educational strategies which are exclusively based on preferences of professionals will show their limitations in other fields as well.

A survey of perceived needs using the format described in this paper can be a helpful tool to investigate problem areas as a first step in starting continuing education programmes. In order to be effective, however, a systematic approach to curriculum construction, using more objective data, is needed. Preferences play an important role in stimulating people to subscribe to a course, so providers of continuing education will have to look at both sides and use their imagination to combine these viewpoints.

Two suggestions from this case study can be relevant in this respect: professionals need to be involved in the organisation of continuing education curricula not only for specifying topics or giving suggestions, but also for psychological reasons to raise acceptance for a systematic curriculum approach.

It is also important to create a learning environment in the curriculum which offers a variety of learning opportunities and, most important, continuity in learning opportunities. In this way continuing education programmes can become a continuous support for professionals to keep themselves up to date in their field.

REFERENCES

Bouhuijs, P.A.J.(1981) "Onderwerpen voor regionale nascholingscursussen. Wat vindt de huisarts er zelf van?" (Topics for CME: the G.P.s´ opinion) Medisch Contact, Vol.36, 599-602.

Bouhuijs, P.A.J.(1985) "Planning continuing medical education for general practitioners: a case study from the Netherlands", Studies in Higher Education, Vol.10, 3, 269-275.

Bouhuijs, P.A.J., de Groot, E. & Gijselaers, W.H. (1985) The implemenation of a continuing medical education curriculum for general practitioners in the Netherlands, paper presented at the annual SRHE conference, London.

Curry, L. (ed.) (1983) Learning Style in Continuing Medical Education, Council on Medical Education, Canadian Medical Association, Ottawa, Ontario, Canada.

Dunn, W.E. & Hamilton, D.D. (1985) "Competence-based education and distance learning: a tandem for professional continuing education?", Studies in Higher Education, Vol. 10, 3, 277-287.

Landelijke Huisartsen Vereniging (1982) Basis-takenpakket van de huisarts, Utrecht.

Laxdal, O.E. (1982) "Needs assessment in continuing medical education: a practical guide", Journal of Medical Education, Vol.57, 827-834.

Leoni, D. (1979) Le dossier F.M.C. Efficacite, animation et pedagogie, Vol.57, 13-24.

Metsemakers, J.F.M., Bouhuijs, P.A.J. & Beusmans, G.M.H.I. (1983) "Terug naar de Ardennen. Een evaluatie van twee nascholingscursussen volgens het Warffummodel", (evaluation of two CME courses) (summary in English), Huisarts en Wetenschap, Vol.26, 189-193.

Neil, M.W. (ed.) (1981) Education of Adults at a Distance, Kogan Page, London.

Parlett, M. & Dearden, G. (eds.) (1977) Introduction to Illuminative Evaluation: studies in higher education, Pacific Sounding Press, Cardiff-by-the-Sea, Ca.

Sibley, J.C., Sackett, D.L., Neufeld, V. et al. (1982) "A randomised trial of continuing medical education", New England Journal of Medicine, Vol.306, 511-15.

Planning Continuing Medical Education

UEMO (1979) "Interim report on continuing education
  for general practice in the member states of the
  European Communities", Report, European
  Association of General Practitioners, UEMO,
  Paris.
Van Es, J.C., de Melker, R.A. & Goosman, F.C.L.
  (1983) Kenmerken van de huisarts II, Bohn,
  Schelkema en Holkema, Utrecht.

1) Parts of this paper are based on Bouhuijs (1985)
and Bouhuijs et al. (1985)

3 PLANNING CONTINUING EDUCATION FOR NURSES – A SURVEY OF NEEDS AND DEVELOPMENTS

Jill Rogers

Four hundred thousand qualified nurses had, by March 1986, responded to a national requirement to place their names on the professional register (UKCC, 1986): four hundred thousand individuals who are either in practice or who, as qualified nurses, may wish to return to practice. In 1985 there were almost 40,000 new admissions to the various parts of the professional register. It is well known that nurses, midwives and health visitors make up the largest staff group listed as working in the National Health Service and that they account for over 50% of the salary bill of the National Health Service (DHSS, 1981a). A discussion about continuing professional education within nursing must be seen against this background of the sheer size of the profession.

Major Changes in Nursing

Nursing, as a profession, has experienced considerable change in the past five years. The National Health Service was reorganised in 1982 and the introduction of general managers in the NHS as a result of the Griffiths Report(1983) has effected far-reaching changes in the position of nurses in the decision-making structure of the Health Service. A new statutory structure for the profession came into operation in 1983. The United Kingdom Central Council for Nursing, Midwifery and Health Visiting and four National Boards have responsibility for all aspects of professional regulation and development.

Changes and developments in nursing must be seen in the context of changing health needs and trends. These are particularly important in relation to continuing professional education as qualified nurses must be able to respond to changing demographic circumstances. McCarthy (1982) has reported that cancers and circulatory diseases are major causes of death in the over 35 age group, and the incidence of coronary heart disease has risen particularly sharply in recent years.

General practitioner consultation data show that after nasopharyngitis, anxiety and depression are the most frequent reasons for visiting a general practitioner, particularly for women. Medical hospital admissions are dominated by drug overdoses, heart disease, diabetes and pneumonia. The General Household Survey revealed that in 1982, around one third of the adult population of Great Britain reported a long standing-illness, dis-ability or infirmity. At the same time, there are major social and economic changes which influence the role of the health professional. Health promotion is being given increasing emphasis. "Care in Action" issued by the DHSS in 1981 (DHSS, 1981b) placed priority on health promotion, and the member countries of the World Health Organisation have declared their commitment to "Health for all by the year 2000" (1981). Nurses have a key role to play in achieving this goal, which calls for education of the public about prevailing health problems, a major emphasis on promotion of health, a serious concern with prevention of illness, and attention to family health.

The Place of Continuing Professional Education

It is argued, and generally accepted, that an interested and motivated workforce will perform more effectively than one which is neglected and disinterested (Houle, 1980; McGuire et al, 1983). It has been stressed that basic nurse education "can only be a foundation" (Royal Commission, 1979), that it should prepare a nurse for lifelong learning and to question her practice (Altschul, 1982). The World Health Organisation (1977 and 1982) has recognised that the expansion in knowledge together with changing factors in the community make it necessary for health professionals to make provision for continuing education. Stensland (1967) has argued that health professionals are particularly subject to changes in the social and economic structure of society. A commitment to continuing professional education has been taken on board by the United Kingdom Central Council who have identified 1988 as the date after which the individual nurse, upon re-registration, will need to demonstrate that she has taken the opportunity to maintain and improve her own knowledge and skills. In addition, the UKCC has stated that this does not just refer to attendance at courses: the individual nurse will need to take some responsibility for her own professional development (Storey, 1986).

The nursing profession shares the commitment of other professional groups towards continuing education: the sheer number of qualified nurses in the United Kingdom means that continuing education programmes should be carefully planned to meet the needs of a geographically spread and educationally diverse group of individual health professionals.

An Investigation into One Aspect of Continuing Professional Education

If continuing education is to meet the needs of qualified nurses, and is to enable the profession to respond to changes in health care needs, educational opportunities must be planned from a basis of understanding of the use made of existing programmes. However, on the whole, limited information is available about the impact, on individuals and on health care, of such programmes. This chapter examines research that was carried out in order to discover the ways in which nurses made use of a particular type of continuing education experience.

Continuing professional education is defined as "planned learning experiences beyond a basic nursing education programme" (ANA, 1974). Included in this definition are courses for which a nationally recognised certificate is awarded, and in-service education or professional development programmes, for which no national recognised certificate is awarded. Between 1973 and 1983 post-basic clinical courses in specialist topics were co-ordinated and developed by the Joint Board of Clinical Nursing Studies in England and Wales, and the Committee for Clinical Nursing Studies in Scotland, and thereafter by the National Boards in the four countries of the United Kingdom. The full-time certificate courses were designed to give a qualified nurse skills in a particular clinical speciality, for example, Renal Nursing or Stoma Care. In the seven years between 1973 and 1980, some 13,000 certificates were awarded to nurses who completed a post-basic clinical course. However, no systematic information had been collected about the ways in which nurses made use of their course, or about the extent to which they remained in the speciality of this course. The main aims of the study were: first, to establish descriptive profiles of the qualifications and experience of the qualified nurses who took post-basic courses; second, to obtain a picture of the career profiles of these nurses after they completed their courses; third, to obtain some insight into nurses´ own perceptions of the usefulness of their courses; and fourth, to explore nurses´ career motivations and aspirations. Overall, the findings of the study contribute to the recommendations about the way in which continuing professional education can develop to be appropriate to the needs of qualified nurses.

The study focused on the certificate courses organised by the Joint Board of Clinical Nursing Studies. These courses, in topics such as Theatre Nursing, General Intensive Care and Stoma Care, are full-time and last from 14 weeks to one year, the great majority being six months long. The outline curriculum for each course is compiled by a specialist panel, brought together by the JBNCS; course centres use the outline curriculum as the basis for a detailed course design. Each proposed course is submitted to the JBNCS and approval to run the course given for a limited number of years. At the time of the study, certificate courses were available in 64 different clinical subjects and in all nearly 300 certificate courses had been approved in a variety of course centres, including hospitals, colleges of education, and schools of nursing. Nurses wishing to attend such a course may be seconded by their employing authority, but the majority would apply to be a course member and, if accepted, would become a member of staff of the authority running the course, for the duration of the course. There would be no guarantee of a post on completion of the course.

A survey methodology was adopted: it was important to know that the study was representative of all certificate holders so that recommendations could be made about future developments. A sample of over 3,000 nurses was drawn from the total number of nurses who had completed certificate courses between 1977 and 1979 inclusive. This represented 60% of all the nurses who had completed certificate courses during this three year period. The sample was stratified to ensure adequate coverage of the eleven main certificate courses, of courses for enrolled nurses and of "other certificate courses".

At the time of the survey there was no live, up-to-date, accurate register of qualified nurses in England and Wales. Addresses were requested from the centres where nurses completed their courses. A 100% response to this awesome request was received although a proportion of the addresses were inevitably out of date. No other sources of information were readily available. Indeed, this situation has not changed radically at the time of writing except that the single Professional Register, held by the United Kingdom Central Council, is a potential resource. A detailed questionnaire was the primary data gathering method, chosen because respondents were geographically spread and a large amount of factual information relating to career paths and qualifications was needed. The questionnaire included both open and closed questions and took around one hour to complete. The questionnaire was mailed to respondents in September 1980 and replies were received over a period of six months. An overall response rate of 64% was achieved; there was a 55% response rate from those who completed courses in 1977 and a 67% response from those who completed courses in 1979. This was not unexpected.

Planning Continual Education for Nurses

There was a difference in the response rates from the speciality groups: for all years, the response from those who had taken a neuromedical neurosurgical course was 84%, whereas the response from enrolled nurses was 47% overall. Nurses are a notoriously mobile group and repeated reminders were sent to non-respondents. New addresses were obtained where possible and duplicate questionnaires were sent to potential respondents. Respondents and non-respondents were compared on age, sex, speciality of post-basic course and the year in which they took their course, and no significant differences were found.

The survey produced a large amount of information about the demographic characteristics of nurses who completed post-basic clinical courses, about qualifications, reasons for taking a course, occupations and specialities before and after taking a course and their career aspirations. Readers who are interested in the detailed results are referred to the Report of the Survey (Rogers, 1985). This chapter will consider some of the main findings in relations to the key issues that arose from the study.

In the ten years between 1973 and 1983 over 16,000 Certificates and over 8,000 Statements of Attendance (day-release, post-basic clinical courses) were awarded. When these figures are seen in the context of the total numbers of nursing staff employed by the NHS, they show that fewer than 10% of qualified nurses possess a post-basic qualification of this kind. Despite the relatively small proportion of qualified nurses with this qualification, they are an important group because of the insight they provide into the motivation of nurses involved in continuing professional education.

Who Takes Post-Basic Clinical Courses and Why?

A brief demographic picture of nurses taking post-basic clinical courses is helpful: 69% of respondents were between 25 and 35 years old at the time of the survey, with marked differences between respondents completing different clinical courses. The majority of respondents, 86%, were female, 14% being male. This is a slightly higher proportion than in the total nursing population where men account for 10% of nurses. Forty-three per cent of respondents were married, the largest proportion 71%, being among those taking Psychiatric courses. The majority, 85% of respondents , were British or British born; 57% of respondents held one statutory nursing qualification, 35% held two and 8% held three or more statutory qualifications. Twenty-six per cent of respondents held "A" Level qualifications: considerably more than the 8% of Nursing Officers reported by Jones (1981). Of all respondents, 31% were seconded to their course, the majority being seconded to Stoma Care, Care of the Elderly or Psychiatric courses. This means that the majority, 69%, of respondents had no guarantee of employment after completing their course.

So why did nurses decide to take such a course, particularly when there is no increase in salary associated with gaining such a qualification, and no guarantee of employment?

> "My job before the course was a dead-end job. There was no way I could use what I had studied in my training. I wanted to continue learning instead of lying dormant and slowly rotting."

> "I lacked confidence and the knowledge to deal with emergences that would arise. I also felt that I did not understand the care and medical management of some patients."

> I did not feel myself to be a fully trained nurse in critical conditions."

Nurses were eloquent in their reasons for taking a post-basic clinical course. The possibility of future promotion was an important determinant for 66% of respondents, the reputation of the course centre was important for 77% of respondents and 84% claimed that they wanted to specialise in the particular subject of the course. Just 29% of respondents thought it was important that their senior colleagues had recommended that they attend the course: indicative of lack of career guidance. There were marked differences in some of the reasons given by the speciality groups. For those taking General Intensive Care, the most important reason for taking the course was the potential use of the subject matter in other specialities, whereas for those taking a Stoma Care course, it was most important that they wanted to specialise in the subject of the course.

Issues of confidence, support, awareness of the need for recognition in a chosen speciality, the need to fill the "gaps" left by basic training were all reasons for taking a post-basic clinical course. It is salutory to remember that fewer than 10% of qualified nurses complete one or more of these particular courses. The needs expressed by respondents cannot be confined to course members. Professional development courses are, at the time of writing, being established in some Health Authorities, but many qualified nurses are still unable to take part in continuing education in relation to these fundamental needs.

What Happens to Nurses who take a Post-Basic Clinical Course?

At the most fundamental level, 89% of all respondents were in nursing employment or studying for a further nursing qualification, that is, up to four years after completing their course. In certain speciality groups the proportion still in nursing was higher: 96% of those who took a Psychiatric course, 93% of those who took a Stoma Care course, and 91% of those who took a General Intensive Care course. Ninety per cent of respondents over 30 years old were in nursing, and 79% of married respondents were still in nursing.

These proportions compare well with nurse graduates. Scott Wright et al. (1977) found that 76% of respondents were in nursing posts five years after qualification and National League for Nursing, in a major American study (1979), 62% of degree nurses were in nursing employment five years after graduation. Nurses who completed post-basic clinical courses were also determined to remain in nursing: 72% said that it was likely that they would remain in full-time nursing for at least three years.

The data also show that there are substantial differences between the speciality groups in as far as course members remain in the speciality of their course. The three courses with the highest proportion of respondents working in the speciality of their course up to three years after taking their course were Special and Intensive Care of the New Born (97%), Psychiatric Nursing (96%), and Stoma Care (81%). By contrast, 65% of those who had taken General Intensive Care were working in that speciality. These findings reveal different course profiles: Stoma Care and Special and Intensive Care of the New Born courses were taken by a high proportion of respondents who had previous experience of that speciality, and who had been qualified for at least seven years before taking the course. General Intensive Care course participants had been qualified for up to three years before taking their course and 68% had previous experience of the speciality. Many respondents commented that they had taken a General Intensive Care Course because they felt there had been a major gap in their basic education and felt the need to gain experience of this speciality in order to be "complete" nurses. Lees (1980) has pointed out that it is difficult for a nurse to move from a position where her work primarily depends upon a uniform response and a reliance on rules and procedures to one which requires the confidence and ability to make prompt decisions that are other than routine. The skills gained on the General Intensive Care course are relevant in a variety of clinical specialities.

It would seem that the General Intensive Care Course, the most widely available of all post-basic clinical certificate courses, is being used as a "professional completion" course by qualified nurses. Again, it is worth remembering that these courses are attended by a small proportion of the nursing profession and we still have to face the question of the opportunities available to those who do not attend such courses. Recent work (Rogers, 1986) has shown that 43% of Health Authorities in England and Wales regularly run "Professional Development" courses. Such courses will, in part, meet the need of qualified nurses to gain increased experience of and confidence in handling unusual and unexpected situations. However, the majority of such courses last between one and three days and it is questionable how much can be gained in such a brief period.

A level of job and speciality mobility is to be expected: Redfern (1980) has shown that staff nurses are a mobile group and are indeed expected to be so in order to gain experience, take further training, or to obtain promotion. Redfern identified what she called a "mobility culture" among hospital sisters where a change of job was intended to gain experience. The study of nurses who had taken post-basic clinical courses showed that 62% of staff nurses thought it unlikely that they would be in their current job for a further three years.

These characteristics of nursing and nurses have considerable implications for the methods used to provide continuing professional education opportunities for individuals. Mobility demands flexibility so that a nurse can continue his/her education in a rational way from one employment to another. Continuing education programmes that are based on principles of open learning, and which relate to the particular, immediate work place of the professional, have much to offer. Such materials are being developed, principally at the Distance Learning Centre, Polytechnic of the South Bank, London, Barnet College, London, and at the Open University.

Career Structure Available

An appropriate career structure is vital to the continued development and satisfaction of individual professionals. Fifty-two per cent of respondents to the research study demonstrated a wish to remain in a post with a clinical emphasis. Redfern (1980) has stressed that ward sister grade is regarded as a career grade and that many nurses remain in that grade for their working lives. Austin (1978) has demonstrated that

> status does not have significance for the nurse. She does not seek work rewards which reward her for the possession of status-giving properties, but she does seek work rewards which reward her for bearing qualities of personal staus.

Of course, it is arguable that in the 1980s nurses also seek adequate financial reward for their contribution. As the Royal Commission on the National Health Service (1979) observed:

> at present a nurse who wishes to continue with and specialise in clinical work will suffer financially.

They went on to say:

> It seems to us that rewards in clinical nursing should depend more on a developing expertise and growing responsibility for clinical decision making than on the responsibility for the management of other workers.

It is critically important that an adequate clinical career structure, with appropriate reward, is available to qualified nurses, and particularly to those who have chosen to take further education in a clinical speciality. If this is not available, the financial and human investment in post-basic clinical education is likely to be wasted.

The philosophy of this approach was echoed by the United Kingdom Central Council (1986) when they recommended the creation of registered practitioners and specialist practitioners whose primary responsibility would be to care for clients and patients. Clinically based practitioners have need of continuing education opportunities to enable them to expand widthways rather than vertically: to explore and develop new areas of interest within the clinical field and to keep abreast of developments in their chosen field of clinical practice.

Matching Continuing Professional Education to Needs

The research demonstrated the importance of considering continuing professional education in relation to the needs of the variety of groups: the nurses themselves, their clients, and their employing authorities.

The qualified nurse has a range of needs: both practical and educational. In terms of practical needs, it is a fact of nursing life that approximately 90% of the nursing population is female: this has inevitable consequences for the profession. Mercer and Mould (1976) stressed that the motivation to stay in a job was a function not merely of what goes on in a hospital, but also what is happening in a nurse's outside life. The research into the careers of nurses who had completed post-basic clinical courses showed that female nurses often have to make compromises between a career and personal life, but that the great majority are committed to continuing a career in nursing. Martin and Roberts (1984), in a major survey of women and employment showed that women spend 65% of their life span in full-time and part-time employment, and that they are, on the whole, stable employees. Flexible, relevant continuing education programmes are essential to meet the logistic and practical needs of qualified nurses. In addition to open learning approaches there is a need for continuing education programmes provided by employing authorities (in-service and/or staff development programmes) to have elements that are mutually recognised.

Core elements of a continuing education programme could be agreed which could carry credibility between health authorities and indeed within higher education systems.

The question of identifying educational need for

individual   practitioners   has   different
perspectives.   The   UKCC   (1986)   has   emphasised that
basic education must

> prepare people for change: to give them the
> foundation on which to build and the
> confidence and motivation to engage in
> professional development as and when it
> becomes necessary (para. 6.52).

The trick is to identify the "as and when it
becomes necessary".

From   the   perspective   of the employing authority,
the Health Service, continuing education programmes
should   meet   the   need   to   ensure   a   competent
workforce   who   are   motivated   to   keep   their
professional skills and knowledge up to date. Every
Authority,   in   its   long-term   strategic   plan,   is
planning   for   a   higher proportion of care to take
place in the community rather   than   the   hospital,
for   an   emphasis   on   health   promotion,   for   the
demands of an increasing number of elderly clients,
and for   changing   epidemiological   patterns.   Each
Authority   must ensure that its staff, its greatest
resource,   are able to   respond   to   these   changes.
They   can   only   do so with appropriate educational
support.

Each individual practitioner has needs in   relation
to   his/her   specific role within the organisation,
and has needs in relation to   his/her   professional
development   and   career   plans.   A   recent survey
(Rogers, 1986) has shown that there are   relatively
few   systematic   attempts   to   identify   need among
qualified nurses.

Performance   appraisal   schemes   had   fallen   into
disuse,   and   misuse,   and were used in just 57% of
Health Authorities. In some of   these   authorities,
schemes   were   operational   in only some units. The
use of appraisal schemes to identify learning needs
was rarer still. Clearly, there is a responsibility
for   continuing   professional   education   on   each
individual   and   the employing authority (Duberley,
1985). Lathlean   (1984)   and   Farnish   (1983)   have
shown   that   ward   sisters   feel   particularly

vulnerable and in need of support with topics such as management of patient care, teaching and assessment, general ward management, communication and interpersonal skills. An effective and supportive appraisal scheme could go a long way to identify and fulfil these needs and to integrate the varying, but complementary, needs of the individual professional, the service and the client.

Major changes are being discussed and implemented in the nursing profession. Increased autonomy and responsibility for individual practitioners; increasing emphasis on the individual's personal responsibility to keep up to date and aware of developments; closer links with and credibility within the higher education system; dramatic changes in the focus of health care and prevention: all have important implications for developments in continuing professional education.

I would like to acknowledge support from the Department of Health and Social Security for the research on which this chapter is based.

REFERENCES

Altschul, A. (1982) "How far should further education go?" Nursing Mirror, July 7, 29-30.

American Nurses´ Association (1974) "Standards for Continuing Education in Nursing", The Journal of Continuing Education in Nursing, 5 32.

Austin, R. (1978) "Professionalism and the nature of nursing reward", Journal of Advanced Nursing, 3, 9-23.

DHSS (1981a) "Report of the Chief Nursing Officer", Nursing 1977-1980, DHSS, London.

DHSS (1981b) Care in Action: A Handbook of Policies and Priorities for Health and Personal Social Services in England, HMSO, London.

Duberley, J. (1985) "Continuing Education: whose responsibility?" The Professional Nurse, 1, 4-6.

Farnish, S. (1983) "Ward Sister Preparation: a survey of three districts", NERU Report, Chelsea College, University of London.

Griffiths, E. Roy (1983) NHS Management Inquiry (Letter to the Secretary of State), The Team, London.

Houle, C. (1980) Continuing Learning in the Professions, Jossey Bass, London.

Jones, D., Crossley-Holland, C. & Matus, T. (1981) The Role of the Nursing Officer, DHSS, London.

Lathlean, J. (1984) The Ward Sister Training Report: an evaluation of a training scheme for ward sisters, NERU Report 3, Chelsea College, University of London.

Lees, J. (1980) "Developing effective institutional managers in the 1980s. Part 1. A current analysis", Journal of Advanced Nursing, 5, 209-20.

McCarthy, M. (1982) Epidemiology and Policies for Health Planning, King Edward´s Hospital Fund for London.

McGuire, C., Foley, R.P., Goss, A., Richards, R.W. land associates (1983) Handbook of Health Professions Education, Jossey Bass, London.

Martin, J. & Robert, C. (1984) Women and Employment. A life-time perspective, Report of the 1980 DE/OPCS Women and Employment Survey, HMSO, London.

Mercer, G. & Mould, C. (1976) An investigation into the level and character of labour turnover amongst trained nurses, DHSS, London.

National League for Nursing, Division of Research (1979) "Summary Report on Americal nurse career pattern study", Journal of Advanced Nursing, 4. 687-92.

Redfern, S.J.(1980) "Hospital Sisters: work attitudes, perceptions and wastage" Journal of Advanced Nursing 5. 451-66

Rogers, J. (1985) The Follow Up Study. Vol. I: The career pattern of nurses who completed a JBCNS Certificate course, DHSS, London.

Rogers, J.(1986) Survey of Continuing Professional Education for Nurses, Midwives and Health Visitors, DHSS, London.

Royal Commission on the NHS (1979) London, HMSO, Cmd 7015.

Scott Wright, M., Gilmore, M. & Tierney, A. (1977) "The nurse/graduate in nursing: preliminary finding of a follow up study of former students of the University of Edinburgh degree nursing programme", Health Bulletin,35, 6, 317-23

Stensland, P. (1967) "Continuing Professional Education: strategies for health professionals", Social Science and Medicine, 11, 661-66

Storey, M. (1986) "Towards the year 2000", The Professional Nurse, 1, 204-6

United Kingdom Central Council (1986) Project 2000: A new preparation for practice, UKCC, London.

World Health Organisation Regional Office for Europe (1977) Continuing Education of Health Personnel. A report of a working group, (ICP/HND/029) W.H.O., Copenhagen.

World Health Organisation (1981) Global Strategy for Health for All by the Year 2,000, Health for All Series, 3. W.H.O., Geneva, Switzerland.

World Health Organisation Regional Office for Europe (1982) Continuing Education for Primary Care, Report of a seminar, San Remo. W.H.O., Copenhagen.

SECTION II:

ORGANISATION BASED STRATEGIES

The chapters in this section discuss situations where education providers or designers have a defined relationship with an organisation (or groups of organisations) that employs professionals within it. These professionals are then addressed not as "architects" for instance, but as national health service architects, or, more specifically, as the NHS architects employed by a particular regional health authority. The education designers are dealing with relatively stable organisations with known groups of practitioners employed within them. Education programmes can then be tailored to take account of features of the employing organisation and of contextual features which affect the extent to which new understandings can be put into practice.

Where an organisation is the unit which is addressed, it becomes possible to harness characteristics of that organisation towards the goal of fostering CPD. Management, for instance, can be called on to give support - perhaps to require - participation in CPD by their staff. The power of peer group learning can be called on via the encouragement of groups of colleagues to develop their own CPD. Most importantly CPD can become an institutionalised activity within the organisation with resources of time and money allocated to it and staff members nominated to organise it. The effort put into the identification of education need by an education designer is then mirrored by similar effort within the organisation directed towards the implementation of CPD.

Where CPD providers work with organisations over a period of time, it also becomes relatively easy to fine-tune CPD provision to the organisation's needs as they change. There is no need to rely on the snapshot in time provided by a survey of professionals´ needs – a snapshot which may become outdated within a couple of years. The establishment of informal contacts with client organisations permits checks on the match between CPD programmes and practice demands: CPD can then go along hand in hand with the requirements of practice.

The three papers in this section discuss approaches which vary considerably in the closeness of the relationship between the CPD providing body and the client organisation. My own paper describes the work of a Unit which was set up and funded at the request of representatives of the client group it served, circumstances which over a period of years promoted a quasi "insider" organisational role for the Unit despite its being located in an educational institution rather than within the health service itself. Stewart Harris discusses the work of a sister Unit set up to apply a similar educational approach to a different sector, namely building design and estate management staff employed by local authorities. The Local Authorities Continuing Education Unit operates on a "fee for service" basis, selling CPD, and selling a CPD planning service to those local authority offices that wish to buy the service. One consequence is that the LA CEU sees itself as starting up a CPD planning process and then handing this over to an office to maintain for itself, with the LA CEU bowing out and turning to the needs of another office.

Ian Lewis´s paper describes a different relationship between education provider and employing body. Here the link is between local education authorities and a university education department offering award-bearing in-service courses for teachers. In one sense these education authorities are also "fee for service" customers (they pay for the secondment of teachers to courses) but the relationship is complicated by the fact that the individual teachers must satisfy certain criteria to be admitted to the course. Teachers are accepted (or otherwise) on to the course on the basis of judgements about their ability to cope with its demands rather than having automatic right of access by virtue of a contractual arrangement between employer and provider as in the other two cases in this section. A tension between the requirements of practice and the requirements of an academic institution is immediately revealed by the paradox that practitioners who might be thought most in need of education may be those who are denied access to the course.

The papers in this section describe CPD provision that focuses on practitioners within employing institutions and in doing so draw our attention to the different purposes which individuals and their employers may have for CPD. Reconciling the aims of the individual with the purposes of the organisation may not be easy. These chapters discuss differing approaches to the achievement of a balance between the two. CPD is not a neutral activity and providers may find education used to some degree as a vehicle for political struggles within the organisation.

My paper describes the educational approach developed since 1979 at the NHS Continuing Education Unit for Architectural Staff based at the University of York, England. This project had been preceded by a study which elicited a list of perceived needs from practitioners: a composite listing based on talking to a (non-statistically representative) sample of the clients in the Unit's remit. However, a contradiction quickly became apparent between the ranking a topic received within the composite (national) list and the importance attached to that same topic within any one of the Unit's seventeen regional client organisations - a gap which became more marked with time. At the same time the potential offered by close working relationships with each of these organisations led the Unit towards the strategy of tailoring educational offerings to the particular requirements of each office.

The Unit was tiny in relation to its nationwide clientele. That taken together with a concern to maximise the benefit that could be gained from the funding put into the Unit, led to a decision to try

90

to make the Unit's service "generative". This was construed not solely as providing CPD, but also as helping clients ' gain educational skills and information so they could develop continuing education for themselves on a self-help basis.

A major concern with the extent to which resources expended on training produced good effects for the health service led to an examination of patterns of educational participation at offices, with the discovery that education programmes were relatively ad hoc, and not linked to concerns arising from the workload. The idea of education planning arose as a means to close this gap between CPD participation on the one hand and work demands on the other. The planning method adopted involved all staff at an office in considering their personal educational needs and interests in relation to those needs arising from the organisation's workload. Management played a part in forecasting future patterns of work, changes in legislation or policy, or other factors that would bring new CPD needs in their train. In the course of this planning process the organisation is encouraged to carry out a corporate review of quality standards, so that CPD can also be used to correct performance deficiencies and to maintain existing areas of success.

To support this process the Unit set up a national network of "education facilitators", one at each client organisation, and has run a series of workshops to help them develop appropriate skills for this role - another strand of the "generative" approach. Underlying this work is the theme that education is a resource, and that it should be managed and planned for best effect just like any other resource.

In Chapter 5 Stewart Harris describes the planning process carried out by a sister Unit, which was set up to offer a CPD service to the range of building and estate management staff employed at English local authority offices.

Although at first sight there appear to be overlaps with the work of the NHS CEU as discussed in

Chapter 4, this account provides its own interesting perspective on the task of planning CPD for a complex organisation. The method developed takes as its starting point Allen Tough´s work on the adult´s learning projects (Tough, 1979) and then seeks to "stitch" CPD in as one of the many learning projects that an adult typically undertakes. From this standpoint the learner´s personal interest and commitment to a learning project are important starting points. The task of the CPD designer is seen as helping learners to identify the moment when they are interested in something, to elicit from learners information that will help the provider to design education that will satisfy that interest, and subsequently to provide education that fulfils these criteria.

However, a corporate organisational perspective on learning projects was also seen as important. Management were asked to draw up a list of issues that the office regularly faced in its work. Individual staff members then met to score the issues on their list according to the importance of each issue for their own work, and according to how interested they would be to learn more about it. These scores were developed into a matrix showing where interest and importance for work coincided, a matrix used to produce a list of the "top ten" issues for each professional group in the office. Management were also asked to put the issues in order of importance for the office.

This unified list of priorities then formed the agenda for a series of short courses. Each staff member could attend three from their priority list of ten, and there was further consultation about the precise content and format of each event prior to its being put on. Staff were nominated to attend their three events by management and the education designers on the basis of the scorings given to topics at the first stage of the exercise. One problem that emerged in the first year was that not all staff "recognised" their priorities in the events they found themselves nominated for - leading to a tighter selection process second time round.

Organisation Based Strategies

This planning method includes the development of an
action plan by learning participants stating how
they intend to put what they have learned into
action - and notes the need for a co-ordinator in
each office to help put into effect these action
recommendations. These education designers hope to
design themselves out of the education planning
process - with the aim that future cycles of
education planning will be managed independently
within each office.

Ian Lewis's chapter discusses a CPD initiative that
is linked to the award of an academic
qualification, a new part-time MA in Applied
Educational Studies for serving school teachers.

The story of the development of this new MA nicely
encapsulates salient issues in the recent history
of in-service education for teachers. An important
theme is the potential tension between the
assessment requirements and educational processes
of an award-bearing course - and the real-life
professional development needs of practitioners.
In-service education for teachers has been much
influenced by developing models within educational
research, particularly by the trend towards case
study and action research methods. As the
implications of these models were assimilated INSET
began to shift away from taught courses which
presented academic knowledge and towards courses
which focused on schools themselves. The
dissertation element of an M.A. course then
provided the opportunity for teachers to carry out
research on their own school-based problems.

This was progress but there still remained the
question of how these new understandings could be
implemented in practice.

The new MA course described by Ian Lewis tackles
this by focusing not on the individual teacher but
on what Eraut (1982, p.11) has called "the
practitioner in institutional life". "Institutional
life" in this case must include not only the school
but also the employing education authorities which
lay down educational policy for their area. They
also play their part in promoting teacher

93

development through a system of education advisers, advisory teachers and teachers' centres - and the secondment of serving teachers to courses such as this one.

The new course entertains applications not from individuals but from teams of teachers, each team from the same school. Individuals within these teams carry out action research on topics related to their school and to each other, that is, individual teachers explore in their research sub-headings from a common theme. The local education authorities (LEAs) are first asked to identify priority areas of policy and development and teams are encouraged to submit applications in these areas.

The "taught" elements of the course are located at "outstations" (centres within the employing LEA) rather than at the University, and supervision of a team's research takes place within their school. University staff aim to act as facilitators of learning rather than as authority figures making prescriptions for practice. Educational methods follow this principle with substantial use of "experience-based discussion groups". An evaluation of the new course identified a few areas where teachers perceived problems, but substantially vindicated the thinking behind the design of the new course.

Some degree of tension remains between the assessment requirements of the course and the requirements of practice: perhaps only an appraisal system which focused directly on professional action could resolve this.

REFERENCES

Eraut, M. (1982) "What is learned in in-service education and how?" British Journal of In-Service Education, vol.,9 part 1, Autumn, 6-14.

Tough, Allen (1979) The Adult's Learning Projects, 2nd edition, Department of Adult Education, Ontario Institute for Studies in Education, Toronto.

4 PLANNING CONTINUING PROFESSIONAL DEVELOPMENT TO IMPROVE PERFORMANCE

Frankie Todd

The National Health Service Continuing Education Unit (the NHS CEU) was set up in 1979 at York University, with a brief to develop a mid-career education service for architectural staff at NHS Regional Health Authorities throughout the United Kingdom (1). This has entailed dealing with seventeen separate organisations (the health authority offices) and the architectural staff (architects, architectural technicians, building, land and estate surveyors, and clerks of works) employed within them.

The initial strategy adopted by the embryo NHS CEU proceeded along fairly predictable lines. A series of research projects were carried out into the educational needs of the different staff groupings within the remit, and these research findings were then used to guide curriculum decisions about the content of subsequent educational offerings.

From the start there had been an avowed commitment to the idea of "office-centred learning" - a term based on an earlier study (Hedge, 1975) which indicated an aversion in the architectural profession to attendance at courses away from the office and particularly to residential courses.

Initially, this office-centred approach took the form of mounting workshops within the health authority offices themselves, and of developing audio-visual and paper materials which could be used within the offices. Later, we began to tailor our educational offerings to the specific requirements of staff at a particular office, rather than offering off-the-peg events. It was perhaps at this point that the term "office-centred

1.The project was funded initially by the DHSS and subsequently by the NHS Training Authority.

learning" began to be an accurate designation from an educational - as well as a geographical - standpoint.

Developing Educational Philosophy

The NHS CEU was by no means the sole educational provider for the offices within our remit, and with only three staff at the Unit dealing with over one thousand clients throughout the UK, we never aspired to this position. The services of the Unit were at that point paid for by central government funding, and free (or heavily subsidised) to clients at the point of use. But authorities were paying market prices to other training providers out of their training budgets. Our aim was to help health authorities to stretch those training budgets as far as possible. It seemed an inefficient use of the resources spent on the Unit if we remained primarily in a provider role, which was so costly in terms of our time that we could not hope fully to meet the demands of all seventeen client organisations. The provider role also jarred with the developing educational policy at the Unit, which viewed successful professional learning as a process of reflection upon practice and the active development of new strategies, rather than as the acquisition of received wisdom from experts.

We therefore began to develop an alternative set of roles for the Unit, in which we aimed to provide the necessary support and information to our client organisations so that they could devise learning experiences for themselves on a self-help and self-directed basis. To this end we acted as educational brokers to help our clients locate and get what they wanted from other educational providers in the market, and set up an information service providing details of educational resources, for instance, audio-visual or paper materials, of relevance to their work.

In this way, we gradually shifted further away from what had been in effect an unacknowledged "systems" stance when the Unit was set up, towards one which viewed professional development as a matter which professionals themselves should direct, and ourselves as facilitators of this self-development.

The source of our funding, mentioned above, is not purely a circumstantial detail. Our awareness of our stewardship of public money at a time when public spending was being cut had already led us to seek ways of extending the educational service we could offer, as described above. In doing so, we were trying to ensure a generative outcome from the funding expended on the Unit, redesigning our service so that it might generate far more continuing professional development activity at the offices than we ourselves could directly provide.

At the same time, the strong concern with value for money emanating from central government policies towards the health service led us to consider seriously the effectiveness of the education in which offices were participating. Resources spent on education for NHS staff are resources diverted from direct expenditure on health care itself. It seemed not unreasonable to expect that this expenditure should produce some beneficial effects for the health service.

How could one begin to assess the effectiveness of education, that is, assess whether learning had any good outcomes in performance terms? Our starting point was the logical notion that the objects of education (for an individual or for an office) should be closely related to the objects of work (for that individual or for that office). We began to look more closely at the patterns of educational participation at the offices, and at how this pattern was arrived at.

With some minor exceptions, participation in learning turned out to be the result of mostly uncoordinated decisions made by a series of different individuals. The "educational programme" at an office was the sum of a set of ad hoc decisions whereby some individuals regularly volunteered or were nominated to participate in education, others rarely; where choice of events to attend was determined by factors such as cost or the attractiveness of the venue; and where attendance at one-off events was the predominant manifestation of continuing professional development. Strikingly, there was little or no attempt to guide participation in education according to the demands of the organisation´s (or an individual´s) workload. These demands were left undefined in educational terms, as if work inhabited one sphere, while education lived in another.

We hit on the idea of "education planning" as a means to close this gap. We saw that it was important to encourage staff at each office to take time to analyse the demands of their work - and then to plan education programmes for each office based on this analysis. This was essentially a content-analytic approach, in which we hoped to make education more effective by helping staff to target it more precisely on work demands.

We had a chance to implement this on a trial basis when in 1981 one of the health authority offices agreed to let us run an "education planning" workshop, bringing all staff together for a day. Agreement was also obtained to bring in staff from other works disciplines (strictly speaking, outside our remit) so that important multidisciplinary aspects of work in the office should not be ignored.

Participants were asked to prepare for the workshop by considering those areas which they saw as important for professional development from a purely personal standpoint. In the course of the workshop participants discussed these personal lists in small groups with their colleagues. They formed into syndicates grouped by profession (e.g. architects, engineers, surveyors) to consider important areas of development from a professional standpoint. Then, in multidisciplinary groups, they evaluated these individual and professional interests in the light of the needs of the office as a whole. In a final plenary session these individual, professional and organisational needs were integrated, and an agreed list of priorities was constructed. This was intended to form the curriculum of the office´s future educational programme.

This pilot workshop was both a great success - in that it promoted lively and committed involvement from staff, who gave it an enthusiastic response - and a total failure - in that the planned educational programme did not materialise. This should not have come as a surprise: no one in the office held designated responsibility to push it through; senior management at the office was under pressure on other fronts and naturally directed effort into these areas rather than into implementing the educational programme; and as an outside organisation the NHS CEU was powerless to intervene.

Out of the success of this pilot planning workshop was borne the determination not to abandon the idea. Out of its failure came the realisation that education planning could not succeed without a nominated person at each office who could work with us during the planning process, and who could ensure that whatever was planned would actually take place.

The Facilitator Network

We asked senior management at each office to nominate one staff member who would take the responsibility of linking with us in the planning and implementation of educational programmes. Coincidentally, we had also been experiencing difficulties over purely local administrative details of educational events that we took out to the offices, so a nominated person to link with would help us in that area also. We used the term "education facilitator" to describe this role, a term which met with initial derision from our clients but which in the course of time has come to be used with some affection. The facilitators were all architects with primary responsibilities for hospital design or liaison work, not trainers or educationalists. Furthermore, some of them were pressed men, not volunteers. Realising that they could not be expected to carry out the facilitator role without support we developed a series of workshops which brought all seventeen of them together on a regular basis.

Starting in February 1983, at the time of writing we have run eight workshops for facilitators. Each workshop has usually had a mixed agenda, in part made up of issues which CEU staff wanted to cover, and in part of issues generated by the facilitators themselves. The precise mix has varied, with some workshops almost entirely given over to collaborative discussion by facilitators of their own agenda, and others (for instance, the first in the series, at which we introduced the NHS CEU´s services and educational approach) having a substantial element led by Unit staff. We produced a follow-up report of each workshop for reference, and gave each facilitator a kit made up of these reports (as they were published) together with other NHS CEU products to help them in their educational role. (These included a one hundred page catalogue of audiovisual materials of interest to health building professionals, and a bibliography of references on continuing professional development in construction-related areas.) The titles of the workshops are shown in Figure 1.

Figure 1. NHS CEU Facilitators´ Workshops 1983-1986

Date   Title

1. February, 1983   Working with the NHS
                             CEU: Establishing a

Common Approach

2. May, 1983   Planning Successful
                             Continuing Education

3. November, 1983   Designing Learning
                             Activities for
                             Continuing Professional

Development

4. May, 1984 Part 1:   Preparation for
                             Organisational Change
            Part 2:   Design Decision Making

5. November, 1984   Counselling Skills

6. February, 1985   Costs and Good
                            Effects: Planning
                            Education to Improve
                            Performance

7. June, 1985   A Review of the role of
                            the NHS CEU and
                            Discussion of Future
                            Areas for Continuing
                            Professional Development
                            for Health Service
                            Architectural Staff

8. May, 1986   New Directions: The
                            Expanded NHS CEU and Its
                            New Clientele

Throughout this period, we continued to offer our educational brokerage and information service, a service which now had direct applications for the facilitators. All the facilitators began to design and mount in-office education, often drawing on information provided by the NHS CEU, increasingly also on tips from fellow-facilitators, picked up at the workshops. NHS CEU maintained a slimmed-down provider role, taking around the country a cycle of workshops individually designed for each office in consultation with the facilitators.

Three Early Approaches to Planning

During the period in which the facilitator network was being set up three of the offices collaborated with the NHS CEU in some form of education planning procedure. By this point in time, there were varying views within the Unit as to the best method of achieving education planning. Since facilitators also had their views and their office circumstances were varied, each of these three offices used different approaches in planning. At one office the facilitator listed all staff in his remit, and then put tremendous administrative effort into constructing a retrospective record of who had (and who had not) undertaken education in the last few years, and on what topic. Topics were listed along the top of this chart, and staff names down the left. Empty spaces at the points of intersection were taken as the agenda for future education.

A second office decided to take one specific theme as the central core of all education in the office for the coming year. The idea was to launch the year´s programme with an impressive one day workshop using big name presenters, and then to follow this up with a series of smaller scale events, each tackling a different subdivision of the major theme.

The third office followed a two stage pencil and paper consultation process which involved staff and senior managers assigning rank numberings to listed topics. The ranking exercise allowed for distinctions between topics thought to be of interest and topics thought to be of immediate relevance to an individual´s work. The analysis of these rankings was to provide the agenda for the future educational programme. (This method was developed by Stewart Harris, and subsequently adapted for use in education planning in local authorities, as reported in Chapter 5. It came to be known as the "Oxford" approach, after the office where it began)

These three approaches to planning were presented by the facilitators in question at the second facilitators´ workshop. However, the main contribution to this workshop was from a private architect (representing a large, multidisciplinary firm with a national practice network) who gave an account of how the firm planned education around quality issues. It had, in fact, been discussions with the firm, and access to their document (BDP, 1979) which had acted as a trigger for the first, pilot workshop on education planning.

The planning processes initiated by the three health authority offices met with varying degrees of success in terms of implementation. One lesson we were beginning to learn was that our facilitators needed to have designated time allotted to the performance of their educational role if their work timetables were not to become impossible. Comparisons made at workshops revealed wide variations in the amount of clerical and administrative help available to facilitators, and perhaps even greater variations in the training monies they had at their disposal. It also became clear that the role of facilitator needed to be held by someone close to the top of the office's managerial hierarchy. More than one enthusiastic but yound facilitator was frustrated in the implementation of his educational plans for his office because of lack of seniority. Factors such as these, and others to do with contextual or political constraints at particular offices, militated against full implementation of the three plans above, but nevertheless progress was being made. Perhaps the greatest spin-off from the second facilitators' workshop was that these presentations from their peers provided a model for other facilitators to follow - and also gave the motivation, with a slightly competitive edge, to get on and do some education planning at their own office. From this point on, most of the facilitators began to make prospective lists of the educational inputs that they planned for their offices, usually using the financial year as a time unit.

The Facilitators' Developing Role

During the period 1983-85 many changes occurred in the facilitator network. The most obvious one was that some of the original seventeen facilitators gave up this role, and were replaced by new faces. We have now had around thirty different facilitators, the turnover being due to a variety of factors (retirements, sideways shifts in responsibilities within the parent organisation) including, significantly, promotions. Perhaps more importantly the facilitators' own activities as they tried out new ideas led to extensions of the role. They became, variously, holders of training budgets, programme planners, designers of educational events. They chaired workshops and small group meetings, hired films and videotapes, booked rooms and speakers and organised educational aids. Increasingly, they also began to have higher profiles within their office organisation. They consulted line managers for their views on the desirable direction of education for the office, and negotiated with colleagues and junior staff who should get release for what kind of education. They were increasingly able to point to a track record of successful education which they had organised independently of the NHS CEU, and this gave added stature to the facilitator role. The themes covered at the workshops were designed to support these role extensions, and the Unit´s underlying aim, to diffuse educational skills and confidence outwards from the Unit at the centre to all seventeen client organisations throughout the country, seemed to be having some success.

Consolidating Education Planning

A major advance on the education planning front arose out of the fact that one of our facilitators was promoted for a three year period to act as deputy chief in his organisation, whilst maintaining the facilitator role. He was keen to plan an integrated educational programme for this three year period to respond to the needs of over sixty professional staff in his division of the organisation and an annual workload to the value of about £70 million. (Staff in other divisions - outside our strictly laid down remit - were also involved in the workload.) We at the Unit blenched a little at the size of this task. This was serious business, not inconsequential educational tinkering. We were being taken at our word that planned education could help to enhance organisational performance.

As it happened, this request came at a point in time when some new intuitions about how education can improve professional practice were beginning to crystallise. We had just carried out an informal survey on two fronts. One was to note instances of failures in practice (mostly as reported in the national press) across a range of professions, and to analyse the factors that seemed to have contributed to these failures. The other was to survey the continuing education available for roughly the same range of professions, and to analyse the kinds of objects to which it was addressed (Todd, 1984). A curious mismatch became apparent. About two thirds of important failures in practice occurred in what might be called the "personal" area: failures in communication, failures thoroughly to carry out proper procedures, or failures to consult (either with clients or colleagues), along with sad but inevitable errors in human perception. On the other hand about two-thirds of the educational offerings were concerned with what might be called "technical" areas of practice: updating on skills and techniques, information technology, new equipment, new laws and the like.

The kinds of costs that were exacted by professional failures varied according to the area of practice, with losses of life, losses of time, losses of money, and decrements in the quality of life of clients being the four main types. Rough and ready though this analysis was, it brought home the importance of using education to prevent the failures that exact such penalties, both for clients of professional practice and for society as a whole.

This work added a new dimension to our aims for education planning. We had begun, in the pilot workshop, with an approach to planning that responded primarily to organisational units within the office: the individual, the professional groups, the office as a whole. The plans of the three offices presented at the second facilitators' workshop, operated largely within a content frame of reference, with choice of topics to include in a programme guided by factors such as filling past gaps (the retrospective record), general relevance (the theme approach) and personal and managerial preferences (the "Oxford" approach). The work on failures led us to seek to add on some qualitative evaluation of past performance on the grounds that helping to avoid their future recurrence was the very least that education should try to do. But we recognised that tomorrow's failures may be of a different kind and have different causes from yesterday's. We therefore also wanted to build in an analysis of the forthcoming workload, so that education could be used in a productive way to assure high quality in that work. The three year planning period proposed to us was a good opportunity to consolidate a pro-active stance.

We worked jointly with the facilitator and a representative from his in-house training department to develop an education planning workshop that would have the twin aims of generating a performance-related curriculum for the next three years, and acting as a memorable launch event to get that programme off the ground. We wanted all staff in the division to collaborate in constructing this plan, so as to enhance future motivation for educational participation. At the same time, we wanted to ensure that their collaboration was informed by realistic information about the nature of the likely work load over the next three years and about oncoming organisational changes, and could also draw on an outline educational strategy taking into account available educational resources.

Factors such as these show how closely education has to link with managerial and organisational decisions if it is to be successful. The facilitator began to make a series of decisions that were in effect laying down an educational policy for the office: relating to how many person/days per year could be devoted to CPD, how much could be spent on it, what proportion of resources should be directed towards helping staff through award-bearing courses and what proportion on more general CPD, and so on. Some necessary areas of training, e.g. learning to use the new computer for computer aided design, were already covered in monetary terms by an agreement with the firm from which the computer had been bought. However, this learning was so time-intensive that for a small group of staff it mopped up all of the time they could be spared for education in the first year. The facilitator was in a sufficiently senior management position to make these decisions hold, and was also able to begin to consider the removal of barriers to the application of what staff would learn in the programme. A substantial amount of preparatory work of this nature was done before the "launch" workshop was held.

The programme of this "launch" workshop is shown in Figure 2. Subsequent NHS CEU planning workshops at other offices have followed pretty much this same format.

Figure 2

* Welcome and introduction to the aims of the workshop.

* Outline of future developments in the organisation for the planning period. (Chief Manager)

* Outline of an educational strategy within available resources. (Facilitator)

* Using continuing professional development to improve practice. (NHS CEU)

* Support available from the local training organisation. (In-house Trainers)

* Syndicate group work to generate suggestions for important areas for education, in the light of the foregoing.

* Report back from syndicates.

* Open forum - to agree priorities for the educational programme.

As can be seen, it incorporated a presentation from senior management about the future directions of work for the division, and an analysis of likely future organisational changes, together with a framework for an overall educational strategy from the educational facilitator. There was an input from the NHS CEU which set out the case for both retrospective and prospective analyses of workload and quality goals, and one from the local training department setting out how they could help future staff development.

Prior to the workshop participants had prepared a list of areas for continuing professional development which were important to them from a personal standpoint. These lists were re-considered during syndicate group work towards the end of the workshop in the light of what staff now knew about future patterns of work, the resources available for training, what the local training organisation could offer, and suggestions about the ways learning could best be planned to support practice. The overall aim for the workshop was to achieve a balance between individuals' interests and the pressing concerns of corporate life within the framework of available resources. The immediate objective for the syndicate work was that staff themselves should jointly reconcile these three factors having been given adequate information upon which to base a good judgement. The syndicate groups reported back an agreed list of target areas for future CPD - lists which were further refined in discussion in the final plenary session. The final list of priorities therefore "belonged" to all staff and had been through several stages of debate.

This workshop was a success in all senses, producing a number of sensitive and realistic suggestions. These were subsequently integrated into an overall plan for an educational programme, which set out firm targets for the first year, and more tentative priorities for the subsequent two years. A full account of the workshop was written up in a document that was distributed to all sixty participants (and to some non-attenders) within a month of the workshop. Implementation of the programme began within six weeks and we are convinced that rapid fulfilment of what has been planned is necessary to maintain the high level of interest generated by the workshop. The programme has been implemented, reviewed as time has gone by (the workshop was held in 1984) and was followed a year later by a similar workshop for all the private consultants who do work for the office, so as to help them also plan education around quality-related issues. The office now works with a firm forward CPD programme for the next six months, and a more fluid one for the next year, and two years.

The facilitator in question was promoted to be head of a similar division of another office shortly after this work, and the same approach is now used there. One of the interesting side-effects of going through this planning process was that it made it easy to set out a portfolio of possible educational responses and choose from among them what seemed most appropriate to the circumstances. For instance, individual learning projects, lunch-time discussion groups, short courses put on specially for a group of staff, day-release to award-bearing courses, have all been added to the programme of half or one day workshops that has otherwise been staple fare at these offices.

The success of this work made it a prime candidate for incorporation into the facilitators´ workshops. We had taken the work on planning some distance beyond the three approaches that had been outlined at the second workshop, and some new appointees to the facilitator role had not even heard that. Accordingly, we used the sixth workshop to give an update on educational planning, with a strong emphasis on appraisal of performance and identification of new and problem areas as guiding principles in this planning process.

A key question in the evaluation of performance, of course, is that of the indicators that one would use to assess it. A handbook on education planning that was written to follow up the sixth facilitators´ workshop (Todd, 1985) sets out some examples of objective indicators that can be used, with a particular focus on those that help professionals gain some idea of qualities of the

Planning Continuing Professional Development

professional activities. The handbook sets out ten
questions to aid CPD planning as shown in Figure 3.

Figure 3. Questions to Aid CPD Planning

1. What budget is available for CPD?
2. What time-period is a programme to be
planned for, and what proportion of work
time can be devoted to training over this
period?
3. What staff groupings is the programme
aimed at?
4. What are the priorities and goals for
the training programme? What is intended to
be achieved?
5. What is the educational picture to date?
Who has been participating in training, and
on what?
6. What resources can be drawn on in areas
such as the following: in-house expertise;
venues; educational materials and equipment
(for example, audio-visual aids); links
with external providers of education;
information about educational
opportunities?
7. How will specific training experiences
be evaluated?
8. What steps will be taken to ensure the
implementation and application of what is
learned?
9. What steps will be taken to conserve and
share new understandings within the
organisation?
10.What steps will be taken to evaluate the
whole training programme in terms of the
extent to which the resources expended
achieved desired effects?

It also suggests sources of information that may be
used to support future-oriented CPD, as shown in
Figure 4.

Figure 4. Information to support future-oriented
         CPD

* Future pattern of work for the
organisation

* Forthcoming new legislation
requirements

* Likely re-structuring, organisational
or managerial changes within or impinging
upon the organisation

* Relevant social, economic, demographic
or political changes

* Technological developments

* Forthcoming personnel changes or
changes in staff responsibilities, for
example, retirements, promotions, new
appointees, students on placement, staff
on secondment, staff with new areas of
work

* Recommendations from professional
bodies, official reports, and clients´
representative groups

Advantages of This Approach

It may be that the advantages of this approach show up most clearly in medium to large, multi-disciplinary organisations with a complex pattern of internal relationships and external responsibilities. Precisely in those circumstances the conception of an overall shared mission is likely to be lost as different organisational units lower their sights to factional rivalries or fragment to follow self-serving strategies. The cry that staff know least of all about the work of the person in the next section is also a familiar one, and one we have often heard from our clients. Against such a background, this approach provides:

* an occasion to bring together all members of an organisation (or units within it) to join in planning their own future professional development;

* a means of balancing individual CPD interests with the needs of the organisation, the professional group, and other colleagues;

* an opportunity for all staff to gain a clear picture of the direction the organisation is going in, and of the part played by different professional and functional groups within it. They can therefore consider their own CPD needs in an informed and non-egocentric way;

* information for the education facilitator and management about the CPD priorities of individual staff members, as well as of professional or functional groups;

* information for staff about available educational resources so that they can evaluate CPD priorities realistically in the light of the proposed overall strategy;

* an opportunity for a collaborative review by all staff of the way the organisation is performing, a chance to share in setting future quality targets, and to plan CPD so as

to support achievement of these targets;

* a non-academic, practical exercise, with a real outcome, namely, the resulting CPD programme.

The final point on the list is a double edged sword. The seminar usually promotes considerable commitment. Failure to implement the programme via appropriate executive action would produce a negative response, fulfilling the cynical prophecies of some staff.

Probably what this approach does is to make possible for a complex organisation the kind of self-review which any committed professional practising alone does for him or her self. Interestingly, on an occasion when attendance at a planning workshop included representatives from small practices they told us that in a much less structured and more intuitive way they tended to use such a process to set an agenda for future continuing professional development for their practice.

The outcome of this approach, when all goes well, is a CPD programme that is targeted (like "magic bullet" drugs in medicine) precisely on those areas of practice where CPD is needed. This makes for a far more effective use of CPD budgets in contrast with unplanned approaches where resources of time and money are expended on CPD that may have no direct relevance to practice.

It is worth emphasising the importance of the education facilitators in this approach. In effect we have used them both as in-organisational change agents and as amplifiers of the capacity of our central Unit. We see education planning as going hand in hand with the facilitator network and with the workshops and materials to support the facilitators. The Unit's strength lies in providing an educational model for client organisations to implement as contrasted with the provision of discrete educational inputs. We could not have developed this approach without the long-term relationship we have had with each of the seventeen organisations across the country.

Relevance to Other Groups

There is nothing at all here that is specific to architects and related professionals. The issue of performance standards is common to all areas of practice, and clients are - rightly - likely to become more vociferous in their demands for quality. Education planning and facilitation can be a way of assuring that quality within a framework that respects both the practitioner´s independence and the clients´ just requirement that practice should not do them harm.

For the NHS CEU, reorganisation within the health service has permitted us to step outside the tightly defined clientele of our first few years. We are in the process of launching planning services and facilitation networks (note the plural) for new sets of clients, in new areas of professional practice. The challenge is an exciting one.

REFERENCES

Hedge, A. (1975) Mid-Career Education for the Building Professions - a study of learning needs and learning styles, Research Paper 10, Institute of Advanced Architectural Studies, University of York, York.

Building Design Partnership (1979) Improving our Education and Training. A Policy for Implementation, Preston

Todd, F. (1984) "Learning and Work: Directions for Continuing Professional and Vocational Education", International Journal of Lifelong Education, vol 3, no 2, 89-104.

Todd, F. (1985) Planning Continuing Professional Development, Planning to Improve Performance. A Handbook for Education Facilitators, NHS Continuing Education Unit, Institute of Advanced Architectural Studies, University of York, York.

5 AN ARCHITECTURE FOR LEARNING

Dr Stewart Harris

The problems of planning continuing practitioner education are not theoretical but practical. It is turning an idea into useful reality that is difficult. This chapter is an account of how a framework for a series of CPD events was made in some local government design offices. The objectives of the exercise were to help the offices to articulate what were the most urgent matters requiring attention, to put CPD dealing with them into effect and to appraise how well it was done.

The keys to the <u>planning</u> process were to help offices contemplate the success and limitations of work they are doing and to draw on the full staff body to clarify the issues these raised.

The keys to the <u>delivery</u> process were to keep participants aware of the relevance of the courses they attend, to notify them of forthcoming events in good time, to help them relate these to their own learning programmes, to identify the learning implications for the office as a corporate enterprise and translate these into action.

Who We are

The Institute of Advanced Architectural Studies (IoAAS) provides continuing education in two ways. Some of our learning events are mounted at York and participants travel here and stay for short periods. These are mainly individuals who are following a learning interest of their own and we call these "away courses". The other way we work is to take Mohammed to the mountain: we put on education events for the benefit of groups in offices. We call this "office centred learning" and its main characteristic is that each event is tuned to meet the particular needs and circumstances of the office. The reason for this kind of CPD is partly economic: it is cheaper because one person travels instead of 25. But it also has two other substantial advantages. It means that the teams of building professionals who work together also learn together - minimising the difficulties of reporting back after a course, maximising the peer group learning that plays such an important part in CPD. It also means that we can tackle some of the inherent dificulties in continuing practitioner education - mainly that it is not only individuals who need to learn, but also the office as an organisation which needs to learn, perhaps by redesigning some of its restrictive operational policies.

Of course, each office is different. So IoAAs´s continuing education units are organised according to sectors: the NHS, small private practices, commercial offices, and local government offices. The sector approach has the benefit that events designed for one local government office can relatively easily be translated to another without needing fundamental rethinking due to differences in the client body´s workload, size or posture. Different strategies for planning CPD become appropriate for these different sectors. This chapter is concerned with local government offices: the Local Authorities Continuing Education Unit (LACEU).

Action not Research

This is a report of work in progress. It is an account of the processes LACEU goes through when we set about helping an office to develop a strategy for its continuing education. This is not a research project, it is aimed at improving professional standards. So the data we are able to grab at as we go about our daily life have the purpose of improving our own performance. It is not designed to prove or disprove a hypothesis we have set and are methodically pursuing.

When LACEU was set up in 1984 we had as a main

principle that we would try to get our client offices to see short courses as a series of related events arising from the priorities of the work they do - not as ad hoc events whose primary reason for being was broadening the mind of an individual. We were concerned with designing a framework for courses and individual learning to take place - making an architecture for learning within which events can be mounted. We worked closely with five offices - in particular, Essex County Council and the London Borough of Lewisham - who together have something like 700 staff in their architects' departments. While the thrust of this work can be universally applied, the particular devices we used have been framed to deal with a large office.

The Client Offices

Each of our client offices was very large, typically having 170 staff. Of these about half are the designers of new buildings or major alterations to existing ones: architects, service engineers, quantity surveyors, technicians, plus smaller groups of interior designers, land surveyors and so forth. The other half of the staff are concerned with the maintenance of the building stock: they are mainly building surveyors and services engineers. The building types are public buildings: mainly schools or council housing but also small numbers of swimming pools, fire stations, libraries and suchlike.

Besides the design and maintenance functions, our client offices are also responsible for briefing the local government committees on matters of architectural importance, and for managing the often very large estates the council owns.

Getting Started

We contacted forty potential clients by mass mailing and followed this up with visits to the half that replied. Some of them wanted to wait and see how our initiative developed before committing themselves; many were content for us to put on a couple of one-off events. Half a dozen were enthusiastic about undertaking a properly planned series of CPD events and since we had a staff of only two people at that stage we decided we should concentrate our efforts on them.

Our general method was to get the management teams and seminar groups of staff to prioritise the issues which needed addressing, and to provide continuing education events dealing with these over a period of a year. Three months into the programme we held seminar reviews of progress in each ofice. These led to some tuning of the programme. At the end of the first year we held similar review sessions, backed by questionnaire appraisals.

Two Precepts

We are guided by two precepts in our work. The first is that people, far from being passive consumers of education, are active learners who spontaneously embark on a wide-ranging series of learning undertakings - sometimes deliberately, sometimes without realising it.

The second is that learning takes place at a moment when their subconscious has processed the data in their conscious minds - the teachable moment.

UNESCO has recognised the first of these and has extensively explored the concept of lifelong education: a top-down model that idealises education opportunities from the cradle to the grave rather than being concentrated in youth (Gelpi, 1979). But it is Allen Tough's work that has most convincingly plotted the extent to which people plan and manage their learning undertakings throughout life: a bottom-up model. His findings are that

> the typical learner conducts five quite distinct learning projects in one year. He or she learns five distinct areas of knowledge and skill. The person spends an average of 100 hours per learning effort - a total of 500 hours per year. Almost 10

> hours per week! Some populations yield
> lower figures, of course, while others are
> much higher (Tough, 1977).

The significance of these findings to continuing practitioner education are twofold. One is that CPD needs to be stitched into this rich interrelated fabric of learning: particular professional studies need to be seen as episodes within an adult's broader learning projects. And in their realisation they need to be tied back to that larger undertaking. The other - much more difficult, this - is to recognise the way in which these interrelated studies come about and attempt to replicate the processes in formulating approaches to CPD.

Central to this is heightening awareness of the formal CPD event as an episode in a learning project that the office as a corporate body is undertaking: attempting to pre-sensitise learners to the significance of the particular study. We see a number of factors that are important in fostering the teachable moment.

The first is that learners should have a broad commitment to the learning project, whether it is a general one (improving the office's performance) or a particular one (for instance, managing the design process). The second is that the relevance of a particular event should be made clear to potential learners - before they attend, while they are participating, as they move into the next episode. And third is encouraging learners to take control of the management of the corporate learning project whether this involves their own learning or causing some change in the operational procedure of their office.

Developing a Curriculum

Courses very frequently are mounted in a vacuum of intention. Notice of a forthcoming event lands on someone's desk and they seek the authority to attend it. While it may be of great interest to them, there are seldom any procedures for assessing its importance in the context of other learning needs or indeed any useful assessment of whether this is the best way of learning about the subject. It´s an ad hoc system. But it does have one shining advantage: prospective attenders have recognised a learning opportunity that relates back to their self-generated learning project.

We wanted to set about developing a curriculum for learning for the office that would retain the advantage of the ad hoc system while dealing with the office´s priorities more sensibly. We thought we should start by getting the office to define the work that it was doing rather than listing what courses were needed: to define issues rather than to describe CPE events.

The Range of Work

We did this by getting the management team to draw up a list of issues that the office has to face. The first office we dealt with did this from scratch. Later participating offices enriched their list by drawing on the descriptions of the first office.

Then we encouraged heads of sections of the office - architects, surveyors, etc. - to distribute this list of issues to staff, who added to it, or clarified it.

The typical list was very detailed but had eleven main headings:

* The public context

* Aspects of the office

* Staff and self management

* Architectural design and detailing

* Design standards

* Documentation and costing

* Project and contract management

* Site works

* Maintenance

* Property

* Other issues

It is important to stress that this is a range of issues isolated by one particular office. We are reluctant to extend such a list to be global. Not only do public offices undertake a different range of work from private offices, but each of the public offices who were our clients had their own personality, their own perceptions of the role they fulfilled, the services they provided.

In a previous IoAAS study of education needs in NHS (National Health Service) architectural departments we had extracted a list of needs held commonly across the UK. Each office still had to relate this to its own work. So the LACEU strategy was to bypass the national study and get directly to grips with the needs of each office (Harris, 1978).

Prioritising

Having generated some kind of broad definition of the individual issues faced by an office, the next step is to select from these the priority action areas. We have usually done this by negotiation between what the management team thought important and what staff thought was: "top down/bottom up". We got all the staff in each office to meet in seminar groups of about 20, explained the objectives of the CPD initiative to them, and got them to score two questions about the list of issues:

The first question: How important is the issue to your work?

The second question: How interested are you in learning more about it?

They scored each issue on a 1-5 scale (not at all important - very important indeed) and we asked each person to modulate their scoring so that there were about ten 5s circled - an attempt to bring everyone's scoring system into alignment.

We developed their replies into a matrix which highlighted the coincidence of each person's maximum interest and relevance scores. An extract from this is shown as Figure 1. This enabled us to take to the next management team meeting the staff's eye view of the top ten topics for each profession. (We generated top tens for each professional discipline since an engineer's list would look rather different from an administrator's.)

Before looking at that breakdown, we got each member of the management team to say which issues were most important from the office's long-term view. Of course they had already scored the chart previously as members of staff. Interestingly, there was a broad overlap between the aggregated staff view and the management view.

So, from this prioritisation exercise, we had a short list of issues to be addressed over the next year or eighteen months. One office's target list is shown as Figure 2.

Figure 1:   Questionnaire Returns

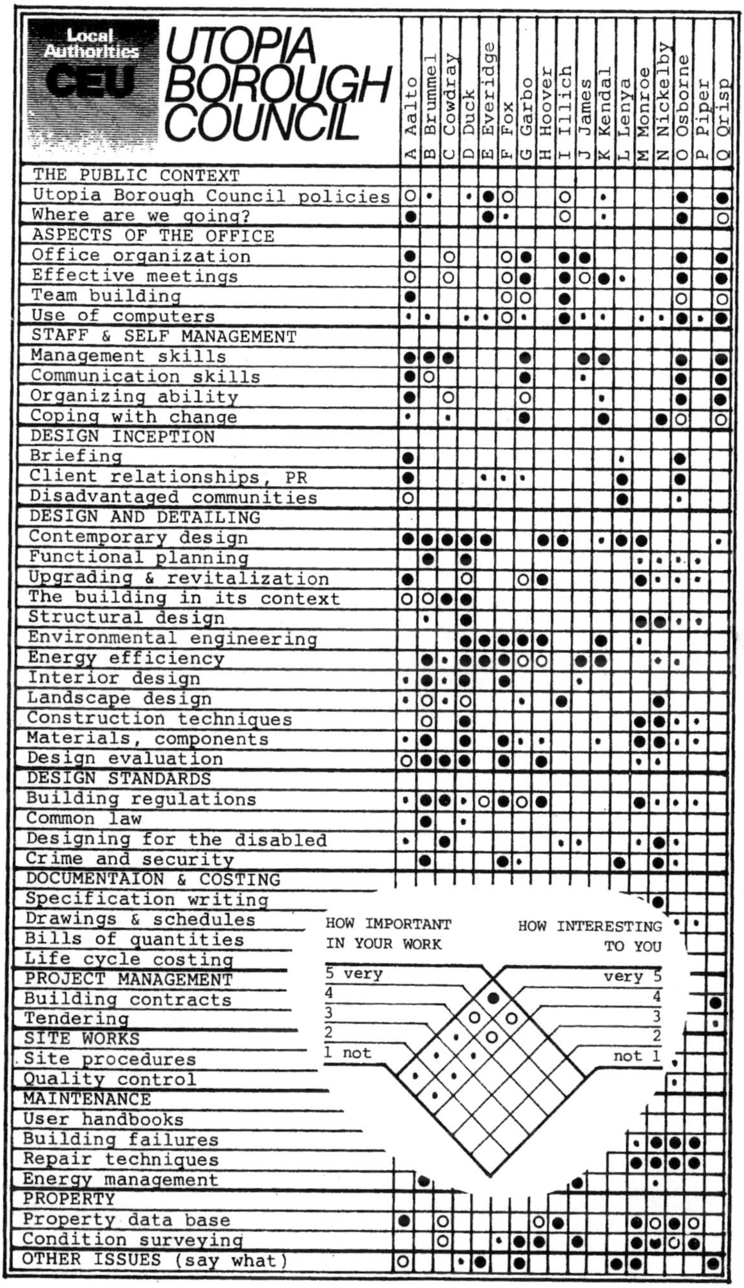

Local Authorities CEU — UTOPIA BOROUGH COUNCIL

	A Aalto	B Brummel	C Cowdray	D Duck	E Everidge	F Fox	G Garbo	H Hoover	I Illich	J James	K Kendal	L Lenya	M Monroe	N Nickelby	O Osborne	P Piper	Q Qrisp
THE PUBLIC CONTEXT																	
Utopia Borough Council policies	○	•		•	●	○		○		•					●		●
Where are we going?	●				●	•		○		•					●		○
ASPECTS OF THE OFFICE																	
Office organization	●		○			○	●	●	●						●		●
Effective meetings	○		○			○	●	●	○	•					●		●
Team building	●					○	○	●							○		○
Use of computers	•	•		•	•	○	•	●	•	•		•	•		●		●
STAFF & SELF MANAGEMENT																	
Management skills	●	●	●				●		●	●					●		●
Communication skills	●	○					●		•						●		●
Organizing ability	●		○				○			•					●		●
Coping with change	•		•				●			●				●	○		○
DESIGN INCEPTION																	
Briefing	●										•				●		
Client relationships, PR	●				•	•	•				●				●		
Disadvantaged communities	○										●				•		
DESIGN AND DETAILING																	
Contemporary design	●	●	●	●	●		●	●			•	●	●				•
Functional planning		●	●									•	•	•	•		
Upgrading & revitalization	●			○			○	●					●	•	•	•	
The building in its context	○	○	●	●													
Structural design		•		●									●	●	•	•	
Environmental engineering				●	●	●	●	●	●		●		•				
Energy efficiency		●	•	●	●	●	○	○		●	●		•	•			
Interior design	•	●	•	●		●		●		•							
Landscape design	•	○	•	○			•		●				●				
Construction techniques		○		●									●	●	•	•	
Materials, components	•	●		●		●	•			•			●	●	•	•	
Design evaluation	○	●	●	●		●		●					•	•			
DESIGN STANDARDS																	
Building regulations	•	●	●	•	○	●	●	●					●	•	•	•	
Common law		●	●		•												
Designing for the disabled	•		●						•	•			•	●	•		
Crime and security		●				●	•				●		●	•			
DOCUMENTAION & COSTING																	
Specification writing														●			
Drawings & schedules														•	•		
Bills of quantities																	
Life cycle costing																	
PROJECT MANAGEMENT																	
Building contracts																●	
Tendering																•	
SITE WORKS																	
Site procedures																	
Quality control																•	
MAINTENANCE																	
User handbooks																	
Building failures												•	●	●	●	●	
Repair techniques												●	●	●	●	●	
Energy management	●									●			•				
PROPERTY																	
Property data base	●	○					○	●					●	○	●	○	
Condition surveying		○			•	●	●	●	●				●	●	○	○	
OTHER ISSUES (say what)	○			•	●		●						●	●			●

Legend (overlaid on table):

HOW IMPORTANT IN YOUR WORK   HOW INTERESTING TO YOU

HOW IMPORTANT IN YOUR WORK	HOW INTERESTING TO YOU
5 very	very 5
4	4
3	3
2	2
1 not	not 1

Figure 2: Who is going on what

Local Authorities CEU / UTOPIA BOROUGH COUNCIL	A Aalto	B Brummel	C Cowdray	D Duck	E Everidge	F Fox	G Garbo	H Hoover	I Illich	J James	K Kendal	L Lenya	M Monroe	N Nickleby	O Osborne	P Piper	Q Qrisp	R Richardson	S Shaw	T Thomas
Time Management		■	■			■			■	■				■			■			
Office Organization	■																	■	■	■	■
JCT Contracts			■															■		■
Project Management												■								■
Life Cycle Costing							■		■	■										
Energy Workshop					■					■	■									
Engineering Controls					■		■													
IEE Wiring Regs						■		■												
New Building Regs						■														
Landscape Maintenance									■											
Defects Round Table										■					■	■				
Construction Physics														■						
Property Review	■													■						
Condition Surveying								■				■	■		■					
Project Appraisal		■	■	■				■												
Design Tour	■		■				■					■						■	■	■
CPE Review	▲	▲	▲	▲	▲	▲	▲	▲	▲	▲	▲	▲	▲	▲	▲	▲	▲	▲	▲	▲
Day Release Training			■												■	■				
Away courses, various	■					■						■	■							
Women's Issues					■		■					■	■						■	

Issues into Events

The next stage was to work up the selected issues into CPD events. The most obvious way of doing this is to mount a series of lectures. But lectures don´t always suit the material to be taught – workshops are sometimes better. And personal learning styles are influential in which teaching methods are adopted. Furthermore, formal CPD events are just the tip of learning. There are other kinds of learning that are the shank beyond this –

126

project reviews, alterations to office procedures and so on. We drew on many different learning models as we proposed a series of learning episodes. The nature of designing education events will not be explored here, since this is dealt with at length elsewhere (Harris and Roberts, 1986). The general method we adopted might be outlined however.

Since our precepts suggest we should relate CPD events back to learners´ relevance so that they fit both with lifelong learning undertakings and stand a better chance of coming at a teachable moment, we were very keen that learners should define what the content of each event should be. We did this in general terms by holding a series of half hour briefing sessions, open to anyone who wanted to attend. In each of these we got staff to pick apart one of the issues highlighted and say what the characteristics of the problem were, what aspects they felt uneasy about, and what office expertise we could draw on and maximise.

The LACEU team took this brief and floated suggestions about events that would meet the need. These weren´t always straight lectures: we liked to use the strengths of the office to deal with the problem nubs and keep both the subject matter and the andragogic methods close to home.

We took these draft events to a management team meeting where two things happened. The first is that in the discussion (sometimes very vigorous discussion) we amended, sometimes abandoned, our suggestions - so we were more certain that we had in fact designed an apposite event. The second thing that happened was that an office co-ordinator was appointed for each event to liaise with us and with the staff who were to attend.

Building Defects: A Case Example

Courses on building defects are among the most frequently mounted CPD events nationally. The most popular format is a one day event in which speakers from building research establishments, university building physics laboratories, and specialists in building pathology deliver papers. There is usually a short question and answer session at the end of each - if time allows!

In the briefing session it became clear to us that great amounts of knowledge about how buildings wear were held by participants. The trouble was, it was piecemeal. Not everyone knows everything, but the aggregated knowledge seemed to us to be very wide-ranging indeed. We also realised that one problem endemic to large organisations is that sharing this knowledge is difficult because staff work in separate compartments. There is, furthermore, very little formalised feedback from building maintenance staff to building design staff. And some of these problems were made worse by professional rivalries between different professions: architects vs. surveyors, for instance. Lastly, some of the office procedures seemed to us to be weak - while there was a theoretical procedure for checking drawings, this was seldom carried out.

Our education proposal was that the issue should be tackled in two related events. In the first we showed teams a simple graphical method of checking designs for water penetration, heat loss and building movement: a method that was adopted by one office as standard procedure. In the second we brought togeher building designers and maintainers at a round table and got them to talk to each other under our chairing. We started by asking, "What are your most frequent failures and how can they be better designed?" There was no stopping the flow of analysis, debate and synthesis that ensued. Our only job was to focus the debate and help clear recommendations to emerge. So the event gave the practical advice that was its rationale. More importantly, it helped break down professional barriers and aided communication: an essential prerequisite if continuing learning is going to be spliced into daily life.

An Architecture for Learning

Who Goes on What

Having shortlisted the issues to be addressed, having developed these into events, we next set about co-ordinating which staff were most likely to benefit by attending. There were three strands to this. First was an absolute guideline set by the management team: there was a limit to how many events each person could attend - partly because of the time away from the drawing board, partly because there are financial limits. This was set at three days per person per year.

Time away from the drawing board warrants some amplification. This is not only a matter of not getting on with the job in hand, it is also an important part of lifelong learning: getting application experience of the formal CPD event by being in the particularly powerful learning environment that is the office.

Allocating those three days was not difficult. Having made allowance for the people who already were undertaking "day release" training - initial professional education - a senior manager and LACEU were in the main able to nominate staff for attendance based on the matrix of their scores. Staff were nominated for attendance based on the issues which they had scored high for how important they were to their work, plus how interested they were in learning more about the issue, as shown in the key to Figure 1.

However, in the CPE review we held at the end of the first year, there were several people who complained about the method of nomination: they weren't sure why they had been selected; they regretted not having gone on some of the other events that had been mounted. This is a generic problem that happened in more or less exaggerated ways in all the offices.

In the most extreme case, we think there were several reasons for the problem arising and one recommendation for eliminating it. One reason was purely practical: two events in the year's calendar slipped back. This particularly affected the administrative staff who were due to attend both. The other reason is not so easy to explain away. The issues staff scored as being of interest and relevance to them often underwent a sea change as we developed them into courses through briefing. So, by the time they were put on, it may be that staff no longer recognised them as clearly.

Furthermore - more worrying, this - people were thrown into the prioritisation process at the deep end, without experience of what our kind of CPD would look like; they were not easily able to grasp the objectives we put to them initially. The relevance of the exercise couldn't be clear until they had felt the temperature of the water. And also, perhaps, we had not been clear enough that, although they may have had ten priorities, they would only have three of them realised over the year.

We think this is the biggest weakness in the planning method - one that persists however much we tried to anticipate it. Our recommendation is therefore that, after the programme is announced, the co-ordinator of each event should meet and discuss with prospective attenders what the event will deal with, why it takes the form it does, and why they've been nominated for attendance. We have since stressed the importance of this updating of intention to all our clients - to set up, in effect, an outline staff development infrastructure.

We had prior to this tried to set up a more wide-ranging staff development process in collaboration with three of the offices' training sections, without success: once because the training section felt the office was not ready for it; once because they were too short staffed; once because of union fears of appraisal being linked to salary reviews.

Out the Other End

Planning CPD doesn't stop when there is a list of courses to be attended, it doesn't stop when staff have been sensitised to why they are about to

attend. The course needs to address the main issue
in hand but it also needs to address another: what
happens next? How is the learning episode going to
be spliced into each person's overall learning
project? And how does the office as an organisation
benefit? how does it learn?

We organise our events to have "action plan" slots:
two of them, kept separate. Through each course we
have started asking participants to keep notes of
what actions they will undertake as a consequence
and at the end of it get them to work in small
groups clarifying these and publicly committing
themselves to them. We also have a general plenary
discussion before the close of play in which we get
participants to make a recommendaton to the
management team of where office procedures need
improving, where opportunities for better practice
lie. This has also presented difficulties. At the
end of the annual review in two of the offices, the
most commonly agreed improvement suggested was that
the office needs to hear these in some better
defined way. Our recommendation here again affects
the office co-ordinator: he or she needs not only
to be a voice to tell staff why they are going on
an event; he also needs to be an ear to hear the
recommendations for action - and have the will to
push them through the dynamic conservatism of an
organisation.

What Next?

We in LACEU see our participation in plannng CPD
very much as a rolling involvement. The minor
reason for this is that we can only work with a few
offices of the size we have studied here at any one
time. The major reason - worth stressing - is that
we are primarily facilitators of learning, not
providers of courses. While it is good for us to
grapple with the problems of initiating a CPD
venture as only outsiders can easily do, while it
is good to set rolling corporate commitment to
continuing development, for lifelong education and
spontaneous learning projects to be really useful,
they need to be planned, steered, and articulated
by learners themselves. Our aim is not to make our

clients the objects of learning, it is to make them agents of learning.

So when we designed our CPD programme we also designed ourselves out of it. This account has been stage one of a process: with us taking the lead, advised and helped by office co-ordinators. Stage two, which is now under way, is for the office co-ordinators to take the lead in designing and managing events with us advising and helping. Stage three, still in the future, will be members of the office taking the lead, advised and helped by their colleagues.

How well this will work, what failures, successes and recommendations come out of it, will be material for a future edition of "Planning Continuing Professional Development".

REFERENCES

Gelpi, Ettore (1979) <u>A Future for Lifelong</u>
<u>Education</u>, introduced and translated by Ralph
Ruddock in 2 volumes. Manchester Monographs 13.
Harris, Stewart (1978) <u>Mid Career Education Needs</u>
<u>of NHS Architectural Staff</u> , Research Paper 16,
Institute of Advanced Architectural Studies,
University of York, York.
Harris, Stewart & Roberts, Norman (1986) <u>Designing</u>
<u>CPD Events</u>, Research Paper 25, Institute of
Advanced Architectural Studies, University of
York, York.
Tough, Allen (1977) <u>Major Learning Efforts: Recent</u>
<u>research and future directions</u>, paper issued by
Department of Adult Education, Ontario Institute
for Studies in Education, Toronto. (A partial
summary of the same author and publisher's <u>The</u>
<u>Adult's Learning Projects</u>, 2nd edition, 1979.)

6 TEACHERS' SCHOOL-FOCUSED ACTION RESEARCH

Ian Lewis

The increasing support for teacher action research within the framework of award-bearing courses brings with it interesting and novel problems for teachers and for those responsible for providing such courses. This chapter focuses attention only on those problems which have been faced by the Education Department at the University of York as a consequence of a major shift in its approach to running part-time, in-service MA courses for teachers.

An outline of the reasons for and the nature of these changes will set the scene for identifying and discussing the problems which are now being faced. While these problems are peculiar to an award-bearing, in-service course for teachers it will be argued that they are generalisable to a much wider range of practitioner-focused approaches being developed in many other professions. This is particularly so since the major problems now being faced at York relate to the notion of enhanced professionalism being encouraged through the course. What is enhanced professionalism? How can it be sustained? What are the political implications for decision-making and professional practice in a world of change? These issues have significance for teachers, but also have wider implications in other professional contexts.

The chapter will contain the following sections: a brief account of general factors which have influenced the nature of in-service provision for teachers since the 1970s; the nature of the initial York MA course designed to meet that new situation; concern for its effectiveness; the current part-time MA course and its salient features; issues arising from evaluation of this new programme; and implications and generalisability of these issues.

Background to Recent Developments in Teacher In-Service Provision

Two major factofs stand out from all those which have influenced developments in award-bearing, in-service courses for teachers since the early 1970s. One is negative and the other positive.

The negative factor refers to the mounting criticism that up to that date most award-bearing courses for teachers were largely irrelevant to the professional needs of teachers. Such arguments were based on a view that the kind of knowledge which these courses purveyed was rooted, to a large extent, in abstract or theoretical material which had only scant connection with the real world of schools. In addition, the course frequently required teachers to memorise this knowledge for later use in closed examinations through which their course performance was measured.

The positive influemce grew from the development of qualitative research within the field of education. This influence was seen to encourage the growth of school-focused in-service courses in place of the traditional kind described above. A particular emphasis within these new courses lay in the encouragement of active enquiry, by teachers, into aspects of their own work. It was generally felt that case-study methods of enquiry were particularly suitable to the need to investigate aspects of the real world of schools.

As these influences began to combine, many in-service providing institutions began to develop courses designed to encourage teachers to examine aspects of their own professional work. Alexander (1980) has provided an interesting description and analysis of the great variety of such courses. One point to note, though, in this development, is the nature of much of the rhetoric associated with these new course developments. This tended to suggest that by undertaking professionally relevant enquiries teachers would <u>naturally</u> enhance their professional competence. In other words, the act of investigating an aspect of a teacher´s own professional world would, of itself, enhance that teacher´s professional competence. Such naive rhetorical flourishes occasionally went even further to suggest that the schools where these teachers worked would, as a result of individual investigations, become centres of enquiry, and that staffrooms would become hives of critically reflective discussion.

There was, therefore, a shift in course provision in terms of the assumptions which lay behind conceptions of professional development of teachers. These conceptions could be illustrated in the pedagogical practices enshrined in the design of courses intended to lead to such development; from professional development through the acquisition of theoretical knowledge, to professional development through enquiry into one´s own practice.

The Original York Part-Time, In-Service MA Course

The Education Department at York developed a three-year, part-time, in-service course in applied educational studies in 1976 in sympathy with these new ideas. The course continues to run successfully - in terms of maintaining numbers, and in terms of numbers of teachers being awarded the degree - with about 20 teachers each year embarking on the three-year programme.

The first two years involve a mixture of taught courses and supervisory support, and the programme has a twofold purpose. Through the courses teachers are introduced to new ideas, and the concern is to explore with them the implications of these ideas for their own schools. Where these courses are assessed this is done through open essays rather than closed examinations. Each essay takes the general form of requiring the teacher to examine issues raised in the course in the light of his or her own professional experience. Successful completion of the assessment requirement allows the teacher to continue into the third year. This last year of the programme is designed to provide for the writing up of a dissertation reporting on the research enquiry which has continued throughout the course under supervisory guidance. Each enquiry is intended to examine some teacher-determined aspect of his or her own professional practice, and the MA is awarded on the basis of the examination of the dissertation.

In the context of teacher in-service courses in the 1970s, two novel features were associated with this course as it developed. One was the decision to use an MA course to encourage and stimulate research into aspects of a teacher´s own professional concern. The other was the development of an overall course design intended to satisfy a number of perceived teacher needs. These included the up-dating of professionally relevant knowledge, concern for the practical implications of such knowledge, introduction to new ideas/skills, e.g., microtechnology, and the introduction to implications of new administrative requirements, e.g.,special education needs. The course also tried to pioneer the idea of concurrency of taught programmes with the supervised implementation of an individual, school-focused research enquiry.

Walker (1985) has indicated that there are a number of dilemmas associated with the design of courses which require a research task to be carried out by teachers. Amongst the complete list of seven such dilemmas which he identifies are: whether introduction to the problems of doing research is via a course or is achieved through experience; whether courses recognise individual needs and circumstances or operate with a presumption of homogeneity about the group; and whether the priorities of such a course are more concerned with academic values or with the professional audience of teachers. In the context of the York course these dilemmas can be recognised, as will be seen below, albeit from an after-the-event examination. The real problem of initiating the programme were to be found more in pragmatic considerations than in those of principle. This is not to deny the significance of Walker´s dilemmas, but it is to suggest that the realities of course design place more emphasis on the exigency of staffing resources; they put a premium on action rather than reflection.

It has already been suggested that the course, in a very functional sense, was successful. In spite of this evidence, feedback from teachers on the course, departmental reflections on experience with it, and contacts with LEA advisers, led in the early 1980s to increasing concern with the lack of impact in the schools from which the teachers came. We became aware that our successful teachers continued to reflect in their research their private and personal interests rather than wider institutional implications. Their research, like their teaching, was being conducted behind closed doors. Our impact within the schools, therefore, was limited by the extent of the individual teacher´s impact and, other than in exceptional cases, this was minimal. We were, therefore, forced to recognise a critical distinction between a successful course and an effective one. A successful course attracts and keeps large numbers of students who achieve the terminal qualification. An effective course, in this context, would be seen to enhance the teacher´s professional development.

Chance conversations - growing out of a rhetorical question of why schools cannot get MAs like Malta got the George Cross - led to a view that two critical features were missing from the structure of this original part-time MA course. These were:

> 1) that individual teachers, like students on initial training courses, are politically weak vehicles through which an external agency like a university education department can exact direct influence on the development of schools; and

> 2) that allowing individual teachers complete autonomy in determining the focus of their research failed to articulate with the social and political context of realisable change within schools and LEAs.

Issues Affecting the Effectiveness of the Part-Time MA Course

We had, by this time, recognised and distinguished success from effectiveness and begun to identify omissions in the initial course design which limited its effectiveness. Further analysis revealed other features of the course which were also seen to limit its potential for enhanced professional development.

A consequence of encouraging individual applications, for example, was the substantial geographical dispersion in each year's new intake. The catchment area for the course lay between Newcastle and Nottingham in one direction, and between Manchester and Scunthorpe in another. As each cohort only met at the weekly taught sessions in York, and their interests varied, there was a major problem in trying to produce a cohesive group. Not only did this provide real echoes of some of Walker's dilemmas, it made further difficulties in trying to promote group interest and concern for each other's issues.

Five changes have been incorporated in a major restructuring of this original part-time MA course into its present form. These were implemented from 1983 and are:

> 1) that applications are considered from teams of teachers who must also demonstrate that they share a commitment to a common area of school-focused enquiry;
>
> 2) that LEAs are invited to identify priority areas of policy and development in order to encourage applications from teams with interests in those areas;
>
> 3) that the taught elements of the course are located away from the York campus to Teachers' Centres convenient for those teachers accepted onto the course; (Because of the use of these Centres, the course has come to be described as using an "Outstation" approach.)

4) that the course is shortened by one year, with taught courses in year 1, and the research completed and dissertation submitted by the end of year2;

5) that supervision of teams´ research takes place in the teams´ schools.

The first two points represent an attempt to ensure a greater degree of support for individual developments. The other changes are designed to encourage greater sharing of interests through a more localised intake, a greater demonstration of commitment of course staff to teachers´ needs, and a concern to relate dissertations more immediately to the research enquiry. The recognition that success needs to be separated from considerations of effectiveness has thus led to major structural changes in the course.

Salient Features of the New Part-Time MA Course

Such has been the favourable reaction of schools, teachers ans LEAs to this new version of the course that, since its inauguration in 1983, the Education Department has already registered its fourth intake and is currently planning the fifth.

Whether such momentum can be sustained will depend on the changes in teacher in-service funding which are indicated in the 1986 Education Act. This factor, in its turn, indicates a major need if effective professional development is to become widespread. This is the need to ensure appropriate levels of support for course provision. Given that resources are not limitless, this also puts a premium on two more factors which can be seen to be critical to the success of such a venture, if not to its effectiveness. One is the importance of LEAs, as the funding agencies, being able to develop priorities and have criteria for incorporating courses into their planning. The other factor requires that course providers operate in close liaison with the LEAs to ensure a sensible degree of compatibility between what is expected and what can, realistically, be made available.

It should be noted here that such a relationship is fraught with dangers, not the least of these being that course providers become the agents of the LEAs. If it could be guaranteed that politicians always made good decisions this need not be a cause for concern. However, there is also the general point made by Fullan (1982) that effective innovation and change do not appear to be very closely associated with a "top-down" model of decision-making.

With respect to the new MA courses one important feature which has now been built into its organisation is a commitment to formal evaluation. This decision emerged from a realisation that only through a concern for the effectiveness of its predecessor course did the limitations of that programme get recognised. THat realisation, coupled with the fact that the new pattern had a number of changes, made it imperative to monitor the new programme.

Our views of the new course, therefore, do not rely solely upon folk memory and uninformed reflection on experience - the natural mode of evaluation in much of higher education as much as it is typical of many professional judgements within schools. The result of this organised evaluation has led to an increased awareness of a number of new issues which appear to be critical to the central question of effective enhancement of the professional competence of teachers. Before outlining these new factors, though, it is important to emphasise the main features of the new course.

It is still, as was its predecessor, intended to enhance the professional development of teachers. It still puts a premium on encouraging this through active enquiry into some aspects of a teacher´s own work. Compared with its predecessor course it now adds the dimension of requiring teachers to be part of school-based teams, sharing a common interest which links their individual concerns. The

141

pedagogical principles on which the course is based incorporate a view that working with experienced teachers requires an emphasis on experience-based discussion rather than an inention to impart knowledge. Knowledge which might be required is to be identified by the teachers themselves as a result of their own needs. The resolution of the course is determined by the report which teachers make on their individual enquiries into their initial concerns.

Issues Arising from Evaluation of the new MA Course

The commitment to evaluation within this new course has already been described. A longer account of all the issues emerging is contained in Lewis (1985). For the purposes of this chapter the concentration here will be upon the three main benefits which are felt to have accrued from this decision. These are:

1) awareness of aspects of the teachers´ reactions to the course which would not otherwise have come to light;

2) a natural source of evidence for helping to make informed judgements about modifications to the course;

3) a commitment to ensuring that evaluation forms an integral function of staff involvement in the course.

Amongst the issues which emerged from the first evaluation - conducted by an outsider and reported in Webb (1984) - were the following: that locating the course close to the source of demand was important; that finding time and combining the pressures of the course with professional commitments were major difficulties experienced by the teachers; that over-reliance on documentation as a major communication medium was not helpful; and that perceived conflicts arose out of aspects of the course structure and pedagogy. These have been singled out here because they are felt to have wider implications for the general area of professional development.

Course Location

It has proved consisently to be the case that the number of applications for these Outstation programmes has been significantly greater than for similar courses run at the York campus. What has also been noticeable is that a very much larger proportion of applications is received from womem teachers. It has often been argued - see, for example, N.U.T. (1980) - that women teachers suffer from a view that they are less career-oriented than their male colleagues. What seems much more likely is that women teachers are expected to undertake a range of personal activities beyond their professional commitments. Consequently they are less likely to be able to take on in-service commitments which impinge on these personal activities. It seems to be the social expectations which surround women in today´s society which conspire to limit their opportunities to follow courses designed to enhance their professional development. Given the key part played by women in many professions as well as in teaching, concern for enhanced professional development needs to take this factor into account when programmes are being planned. On our evidence location of the course is one straightforward way of ensuring that it impinges as little as possible into the extra-professional time of the individual.

Time and Pressure

The advantage of a part-time course is that quite naturally it can require the focus of concern and enquiry to be upon some aspect of a teacher´s work. The disadvantage is that such enquiries have to be added to the demands of the professional activity itself. To gain the benefits makes substantial additional demands on time. These demands are compounded when the course within which they take place is award-bearing. This is because the criteria, which govern the decision about the award, are likely to be based on assessment demands. That such demands can be met is indicated by the success rate within the programme. That they can also figure in the drop-out rate is something which cannot be denied.

The situation highlights a problem for any institution of higher education where a significant element of funding arrangements is tied to student numbers on award-bearing programmes. Alternative sources of funding might reduce this problem, by reducing the need to offer formal awards. However, the "Catch 22" in the situation, especially for teachers, is that the terminal award is a major inducement to participation in the programme. Advanced qualifications are felt to play an important part in enhancing career prospects.

Communication

Great care was, and continues to be, taken in outlining course expectations, organisation, content and procedures. These aspects were well documented and copious papers were distributed. These documents covered such issues as the inter-relatedness of the various elements of the course, the nature, intention and organisation of the assessment requirements. In every case the subsequent evaluation turned up clear indications that the intended messages had either not been received, or else that the teachers' experiences on the course had given them alternative messages.

Clarity of communication has to be seen as another aspect of the time-pressure equation. Too much can be attempted too soon, and the results can be the opposite of what is intended. Rather than making a complex situation easier to comprehend and cope with, communication can make it appear even more complicated. Within our programme we are still not sure we have got the right answers to this problem, but in recognising its existence we are taking deliberate steps, with each new intake, to improve on past procedures.

Structure and Pedagogy

What evaluation has also identified is another important source of contradiction. This lies in the tension between the stated aims of the course and the aims which might be implied in the pedagogical practices through which the aims are to be achieved. Further evidence of the continuing existence of this problem has been provided in the latest, in-house, evaluation report, (Munn, 1986).

Examples of this contradiction would include the participants' frequently stated expectation that course staff are authorities whose comments are taken to have prescriptive force. This contrasts with a staff position that their role is essentially that of facilitator, functioning as encouraging further thinking on an issue.

Another example is to be found in the reactions to views expressed by supervisors, whose concern is with supporting the individual and team projects, as compared with the views seen to emerge from experience of staff associated with the taught programme. Confusion sometimes arose in this connection particularly in relation to the taught programme designed to introduce all the teachers to general problems of research into aspects of their own practice.

Further issues to emerge relate to the general problem of adult learning in the particular context of a course designed to enhance professional development. Mention has already been made of an overall commitment to encourage discussion and a concern to relate course content directly to the teachers' professional experience. Translating these principles into course practice is not at all straightforward. Two factors contribute to the complications here. One is a consequence of wanting to ensure as wide a spread as possible of educational experience within each course intake. We usually have teachers from all kinds of school, ranging between Infant and Sixth Form, as well as teachers in further educaton, and we have had teams from the schools advisory service and other support services. The other aspect of diversity is reflected in the areas which teams take as their general concern for enquiry. Such diversity gives real substance to one of Walker´s dilemmas already referred to - the dilemma between recognising the individual circumstances and needing, perhaps, to treat the group in some respects as homogeneous.

Evaluation has forced us to recognise the real existence of these problems and made us attempt to explore ways in which their effects can be minimised. Without the impetus which evaluation reports provide, it could be all too easy not to recognise the significance of these issues to the overall effectiveness of the course, and rely solely on the criteria of success already noted.

However, in addition to these functional benefits, it is also worth re-emphasising an earlier point about the value of formal evaluation in the context of this section. The course is predicated on a commitment to enhanced professional understanding for teachers. It is not designed on principles of imparting a priori knowledge. This does put a premium on staff being reactive to the teachers´ needs. It follows that course staff also have to be concerned for their own professional development. In this respect formal evaluation can play as large a part for course staff as it is intended to do for the teachers.

At the same time it must be admitted that the addition of a commitment to formal evaluation to the routine tasks of running the course presents the staff with exactly the same kinds of pressures already identified for the teachers. The most important of these is the pressure on time which adding new demands must always create. Against this, though, has to be set the undoubted advantages, which include the awareness of factors which limit the effectiveness of the course and which can be modified. These advantages also serve to confirm the principle that critical enquiry into one´s own work can enhance the understanding of how it can be improved.

Implications and Generalisations to the Field of Continuing Education

The bulk of this chapter has so far been concerned to describe the development and salient features of a relatively novel approach to encouraging enhanced professional development for teachers. It operates within an institutional framework and leads to the award of an MA. The present course has grown out of an earlier approach which was eventually found to be less effective in promoting professional development and providing support for continuing school-based change. In this concluding section it is intended to raise issues which are felt to have a wider relevance than the context of in-service training for teachers in which they have originated.

These issues are to do with working with experienced adults, the critical nature of the location and structure of professional education courses, the implications of different ways of recognising successful completion of a professional development course, and the major problem of identifying effectiveness for such courses.

Working with Experienced Adults

In the world of teacher education it is highly likely that those involved in running courses for experienced teachers have also been involved in the initial training of new teachers. They are also likely to have been school teachers themselves. The problem that this can create, and which is felt to be relevant to many other occupational areas, is that success in one area of work is no guarantee of success in another. Being a good teacher does not automatically provide a basis for becoming a good trainer of new teachers, nor for offering effective encouragement to experienced teachers. There are two issues here. One is concerned with authority, and the other relates to the problem of increasing the effectiveness of experienced practitioners.

In the first case there is a need to recognise that

the basis for accepting the authority of a trainer will be different where training is focused on new entrants from the situation likely to apply when working with already experienced professionals.

In the second case the issue seems to turn on whether the trainer role is seen to involve a prescriptive stance - knowing what should be done and seeing continuing professional education as the vehicle for imparting this knowledge. The alternative model, embedded in the approach adopted in the in-service course for teachers already described, involves a different stance. This approach entails a view that what is important is facilitating the recognition, by experienced teachers, of critical factors which affect their own effectiveness.

A major principle in the design of the course described here has been the idea that innovation and development within a school are most likely to take place where there is a commitment on the part of those involved to the need for change. Only when this necessary condition exists will it follow that analysis of the situation will form an effective basis for decisions about appropriate developments and their eventual implementation. In this view we are consistent with the analysis of change and development elaborated by Fullan (1982): that innovation, change and development in schools are not effective if they are imposed from the top down. It is asserted here that such a situation is likely also to be characteristic of many other occupational situations.

From this standpoint we are left with the view that courses which are designed to improve practitioner performance require, on the part of the practitioner, a developed awareness of the context in which the job is undertaken. This will not, in many cases, occur naturally through experience of the job, or at least without some form of direct encouragement. The need for courses at all, therefore, has the beginnings of a justification. Their continued acceptability will lie in the eventual acceptance by practitioners that there is a demonstrable benefit to them from participation

148

in such programmes.

To take their own definitions of their problems as a starting point in these courses is, on the basis of our experience with teachers, an effective way of working towards the eventual accepance of the need for analysis and evaluation of ensuing developments. Such a stance, as has already been seen, carries with it an important pedagogical principle - the denial of the relevance of a detailed, a priori corpus of knowledge to all the kinds of problems which practitioners can identify. The need is thus established for the design of courses to promote enhanced professional development to start from where the practitioners themselves feel they are.

The further factor which makes this approach to continuing professional education so necessary is the recognition of the age and experience of those who are likely to take such courses. They are adults with substantial experience. It is unlikely that they will take kindly to, or be influenced by, courses which operate on principles of teaching and learning more appropriate to children or novices in the field.

Location and Course Structure

The first of these issues has already been dealt with at some length earlier in the chapter. It was argued that there needs to be a substantial expansion of professional development courses, run on a part-time basis, located near to centres of demand. This is likely to be true for a range of professions as well as for teaching, as other contributors to this book demonstrate. Such an approach will allow courses to relate more obviously to professional experience and practice. They will also encourage the greater involvement of more women in professional development programmes.

The implicatons of working with experienced adults already mentioned, and the implications of locating courses near occupational centres of demand, need to be considered in relation to the structure of such courses. The point has already been made about the underlying pedagogical principles of course design and the assumptions that staff need to bring to these courses. The final issue to be raised in this section relates to the set of aims which such courses are intended to achieve. A stated commitment to developing enhanced professional understanding, for example, will not be achieved without substantial thought as to what is meant and how the content and organisation of any course are demonstrably able to promote such an aim.

The evidence of the main part of this chapter has provided insight into how a particular kind of course has been developed in order to achieve this aim for experienced teachers. While different occupations will impose different demands by their very nature, the need for detailed concern with all aspects of the structure of courses aimed at experienced practitioners will be common to all areas. From our experience we would wish to insist upon a commitment to formal course evaluation as an essential part of the involvement of staff in the provision of these courses. Again we see this as being relevant to all areas of professional activity.

Identifying Effectiveness

It can be argued that we are becoming a qualification-oriented generation. Within teaching there is much evidence to indicate that acquisition of further qualifications can assist with career prospects, even if it cannot guarantee promotion. However, the existence of a need for formal qualifications does create problems for the effective implementation of courses designed to enhance professional development.

Put most simply this is because, in meeting assessment requirements necessary to determine the award of qualifications, we add another demand to those already being met. This raises two questions.

Where occupations involve practical behaviour, is it consistent with enhanced professional development to assess such develoment through more traditional, predominantly written, forms of evaluation?

If occupational understanding is to be based on informed analysis of the context of practice, can this really be shown to have taken place without the production of a series of written accounts of critical issues containing evidence of how the practitioner´s views have changed?

It has already been pointed out how easy it is to confuse the success of a course with its effectiveness. Such confusion can be made worse when qualificatons are associated with completion of a course. Evidence of demand and entry to the course, coupled with measures of successful achievement of terminal qualifications, can easily blind those responsible to the fact that none of these provides any demonstrable indications that professional development has occurred.

The critical point, then, is not so much to do with whether association of qualifications with professionl courses is a bad thing. The reality of the world in which such courses must be run, and the reality of the world in which professionals operate, suggest that qualifications are more likely to be in demand than not. The issue, then, is that of ensuring the compatibility of assessment demands with the activities through which the course intends to encourage professional development. We are already moving substantially towards that in our in-service courses for teachers, and presume that similar developments are possible within other occupational areas.

Afterword

It would be improper to conclude this chapter with the above discussion because there is one further point to emerge from our experience with teachers which also bears on general notions of enhanced professional development.

One reason why courses are required is, presumably,

because of a view that the place of work is, of itself, incapable of providing the right climate of support and encouragement for the professional development of practitioners. It must, however, be recognised that contact between facilitators and professionals only takes place for the duration of any course. After this the practitioners are left to their own devices, albeit with an enhanced capacity for more effective operation, within these same inhospitable institutions. The notion of team registration for our teacher courses is one way of moving towards overcoming this fact of professional isolation. Of itself, though, this cannot be sufficient to ensure that the place of work is transformed into a more professional context for the support of individual development.

What seems to be required, then, goes beyond the provision of continuing education programmes. There is a patent need to ensure that these courses are only the start of the development of closer and continuous association between practitioners and course providers. In saying this, though, it is recognised that little has been done save the identification of a need; it will take another chapter, in another book, to explore the extra questions which these further developments raise.

REFERENCES

Alexander, R. (1980) "Towards a Conceptual Framework for School-focused Inset", British Journal of In-Service Education, 6,3, 137-142.

Fullan, M. (1982) The Meaning of Educational Change, Ontario Institute for Studies in Education, Toronto.

Lewis, I. (1985) Teacher Action Research and Award Bearing Courses: A Coarse Organiser's View, paper presented at the annual conference of the British Educational Research Association, Sheffield, August 1985. (Copies are available from the author at the Education Department, University of York, England.)

Munn, P. (1986) Teachers Perceptions of Year One of the Outstation Programme: Bramley Grange Cohort 1984-85, Education Department, University of York, England.

N.U.T. (1980) Promotion and the Woman Teacher, NUT/EOC, London.

Walker, R. (1985) Doing Research, Methuen, London.

Webb, R. (1984) An Evaluation of the Cleveland Outstation Programme, Education Department, University of York, England.

SECTION III:

PRACTITIONER BASED APPROACHES

The two previous sections have dealt with methods of planning CPD that address groupings of professionals: the whole profession in Section One and within employing organisations in Section Two.

This section focuses upon individual practitioners and looks at ways to encourage individual reflection upon the quality of practice and upon desirable directions for professional development.

The best justification for this individual focus is that in the final analysis it is a series of individual actions that constitute professional practice. These chapters direct our attention to the fine grain of personal histories and attitudes that are the origins of professional action. They reveal the person behind (within) the professional and suggest that it is this person who should be the focus for development.

But individuals are unique – and this starting point leads to quite different ways of planning CPD from those discussed in the previous sections. No individual is deemed to be able to stand as surrogate for other individuals: so survey research and sampling methods are inappropriate. Individuals have past histories and futures in which they can decide upon new courses of action: so primacy is given to the consistent thread of an individual´s past history of learning and professional practice as it entwines into the present, rather than to the immediacy of the organisational context in which the professional works. Here we are looking at one-to-one working where a CPD designer or researcher joins with an individual practitioner to support a process of self-evaluation – and self-revelation.

The task of the CPD designer, viewed from this perspective, is to provide an occasion and to act as catalyst for such reflection. These final three chapters describe different ways of achieving this. In one case researchers used a series of interviews to elicit professional life histories; in another a microcomputer program is used to assist a general appraisal of an individual's performance against criteria set by that same professional; in another professionals are helped to use a personal audit of their past learning and experience in order to make decisions about future learning.

Running through each of these chapters is a belief in the individual's capacity for change; the Rogerian model, which would suggest professionalism is a process of becoming rather than an achieved state, is close at hand. They are each also predicated upon a belief in the individual's professional autonomy and provide examples of ways of working aimed at reinforcing that autonomy.

These chapters also draw attention to the critical nature of the relationship between a professional and the consultant with whom the professional is working. This theme is common throughout the book but the consideration of a relationship between one and one throws the issue into sharp relief. Another important issue is shadowed behind it in the argument that the qualities of the relationship between CPD consultant and professional should model the qualities of an ideal relationship between professional and client.

Peter Woods and Pat Sikes describe the use of teacher biographies - a method of working which is conceptually related to the use of teacher action research as discussed in Chapter Six. Action research asks professionals to make their own practice the object of a disciplined enquiry, using as data information and observations gained in the course of their practice. The results of such an enquiry may be too context-tied to be generalisable; but they do support a detailed evaluation by a professional of a chosen aspect of practice.

Practitioner Based Approaches

Action research calls upon qualitative techniques of social and educational enquiry such as participant observation and case study methods. It is a method that focuses upon what the practitioner does now because one cannot go back in time to carry out direct observations on one's practice. But reflection on practice may be encouraged by other means without requiring practitioners to carry out research. The practitioner is a person with a history and a past career that has helped to affect what s/he is in the present and which influences what s/he will be in the future. Biographical methods can be used both to explore this history and to prompt a reappraisal by a professional of the direction in which s/he is travelling.

Such a "life history" or "assisted autobiography" may be constructed in the course of a series of one-to-one interviews between researcher and professional as described in Chapter Seven. The original focus of this research study was an interest in teachers' subjective experience of their careers, but Pat Sikes and Peter Woods show how in offering the opportunity for "instructive, cathartic and therapeutic reappraisal" the method can be used for self-evaluation and thus to support professional development.

The aided autobiography reveals the level of personal engagement a professional may bring to practice, and helps to trace back to their roots the particular aspects of self that are given expression in professional life. The method provides a means for teachers to confront their own practice, perhaps via the recounting and examination of critical incidents from a career. This process of self-discovery, it is argued, provides the kind of cathartic shock that is necessary to promote attitude change; but the important point is that this "shock" is derived from the teacher's own discoveries, not imposed from outside. This focus on the teacher remaining in control is important; to assist an autobiography is not by any means the same endeavour as writing a biography. By appreciating the teacher as a professional, the method provides a safe space professional, the method provides a safe space within which teachers can review their classroom practice. In responding to the teacher as a person it also provides a degree of confirmation of the person that may be sustaining and empowering.

The "aided autobiography" does not require individuals to carry out the operations of social enquiry called for by action research, but it does draw on the explanatory power of educational and social science concepts. Setting everyday critical incidents within a general framework of understanding provides a means of dealing with some of the stress that they produce, in the sense that to make sense of an event is no longer to be at its mercy. Peter Woods and Pat Sykes refer to this process as "living sociology". As a result of constructing an understanding of, for instance, the effect of social class background or gender upon their own lives, teachers may go on to monitor teaching materials and their own interactions for negative preconceptions that might be damaging to pupils.

In Chapter Eight we shift to a direct appraisal of performance itself. Terry Keen rightly points out that the appraisal of performance is an issue that will not go away - but he rejects as inappropriate behaviourally oriented methods of appraisal, which set up external standards and assess professionals against them. Effectiveness is not something that develops in a vacuum but pertains to the way a particular professional deals with particular clients. The uniqueness of each client and the variations between them suggest that behavioural checklists of effectiveness may miss the mark: what is effective with one client may not be so with another.

Instead Terry Keen suggests that professionals (in this case, teachers) can be helped to construct or express their own set of criteria for effective performance, and to appraise themselves against them. The mechanism to elicit these criteria is an interactive microcomputer program (FLEXIGRID) based on personal construct theory and repertory grid techniques.

Can a machine perform the function of facilitating reflective self-appraisal? Keen suggests that interfacing with the program provides a privacy which many teachers value - and it is designed so that it can if wished be used without any other human help. The program sets up a dialogue in which teachers first enter into the computer variables which they feel are important for effective teaching - and then compare themselves and other teachers against these ideals. The results of these reflections are printed out so that the teacher receives graphical representations of where s/he has placed herself in relation to others, and of the range of teaching skills s/he possesses in relation to the set of skills s/he has suggested is desirable. The program's questions prompt a series of explicit statements about professional practice. What would otherwise have been fleeting intuitions are transformed on the printouts into examinable form - with the constant facility to revise or feed in additional variables. Teachers can build up as complicated a model of their own professional practice as is desired; the program has the capacity to peform many operations upon the raw data so that the "mirror" upon practice which the program affords can be placed to reflect from different angles.

Many teachers choose to have help from a consultant in interpreting the results of their interaction with the program, and then the consultant's more sophisticated understanding of the program and its operations permits a more detailed appraisal against richer models. Here again we find an emphasis on the effects of the quality of the relationship between professional and consultant for the way the results are construed, an emphasis on the need for co-operation, openness and trust.

One of the fascinating features about FLEXIGRID is the potential it offers to conceptualise movement - movement from a non-ideal state towards the ideal - which can lead on to "behaviour experiments" where a teacher tries desired skills. This parallels at a specific behavioural level the notion of personal growth and change which Peter Woods and Pat Sikes used to inform their "assisted autobiographies".

John Cowan and Anna Garry take us into the arena of designing learning programmes that can respond to an individual professional's needs. The professionals discussed in Chapter Nine were mature engineers seeking chartered status or younger engineers preparing for a professional interview. Each of these hurdles poses some problems, it seems, not the least that preparation for them is usually carried out alone rather than as a member of a group or within an educational institution. Candidates need to have a good understanding of what the requirements of the assessment are - but equally they need to have a good understanding of their own abilities so as to set themselves an appropriate programme of self-development. Essentially they need to audit their own strengths and weaknesses in relation to what assessors will be looking for, and then to take steps to turn weaknesses into strengths well in advance of assessment procedures.

One potential educational response to this group would have been simply to run courses on a series of skill areas relevant to the assessment: on current topics of interest to practice, in the case of those preparing for a professional interview, perhaps, or on report-writing or information-seeking skills for those preparing the ten thousand word thesis for admission towards gaining chartered status.

John Cowan's and Anna Garry's rejection of this sraightforward standard provider-based model derives from their view of learning, which suggests that prior learning influences subsequent learning. It is therefore pointless to offer courses "off the peg". A first and important task is to discover the nature of the prior learning that has taken place. Only then can educational activities be designed which respond to each individual's previous engineering experience, to preferred learning styles and to those personal characteristics which affect learning.

It is suggested in this chapter that the diagnosis

of one´s own learning needs may be a tougher
assignment than carrying out learning to meet those
needs. John Cowan and Anna Garry saw themselves as
facilitators of this process of self-appraisal,
taking time to develop a relationship with each
individual and following the Rogerian model of
facilitation: questioning, mirroring and also,
importantly, guarding insights from being
forgotten. After initial sessions with individual
professionals there would then be some group
meetings for those with shared aims and similar
patterns of learning. The lengthy individual
discussions helped to set the agendas for a
programme of workshops in which the learning
activities devised responded directly to
aspirations expressed in the individual interviews.

The heart of this approach is that professionals
diagnose their own learning needs. Facilitating
this process calls for one-to-one working that is
expensive in terms of time – but rewarding for the
professionals and, it seems, valuable in terms of
their performance in professional assessments.

7 THE USE OF TEACHER BIOGRAPHIES IN PROFESSIONAL SELF-DEVELOPMENT

Peter Woods and Patricia J. Sikes

Teacher Careers and LIfe Histories

Teaching is stressful, hectic, imperfect, all-consuming (Kyriacou and Sutcliffe, 1979; Dunham, 1980; Roy, 1983) The teaching day may be fragmented, discontinuous, at the mercy of change. Teachers´ careers, increasingly, are becoming difficult to define and to realise as the profession declines in status and as opportunities for promotions diminish. Both in terms of the efficacy of one´s teaching and of one´s own career, there would appear to be great need currently for teachers to reflect and to rethink on a systematic basis (Pollard, 1985). There are massive individual adjustments that have to be made if the radical changes that are currently affecting the profession are to be successfully negotiated.

We are concerned here, therefore, with <u>subjective</u> careers (Hughes, 1937) - with how <u>individuals</u> themselves perceive and make sense of what is happening to them. While this certainly involves to some extent a reconsideration of formal career progress through objective channels, it also includes more detailed consideration of the job one currently does and how it is done, since one is likely to continue to be in the same position for much longer than might have been expected before the 1980s crisis. Following on from this is a reappraisal of what is put into and got out of teaching - i.e. job satisfaction.

Clearly, teachers themselves are their own best resource in this activity (see also Smyth, 1982). They need, however, a method to make the best use of this resource, as well as time in which to use it. Several forms of "action" and "collaborative" research have proved helpful here (Stenhouse, 1975; Nixon, 1981; Hustler et al., 1986; Sikes, 1986). The "illuminative", "qualitative" or "ethnographic" research techniques which have become popular in educational research in recent years are also readily accessible to teachers (Woods, 1985b, 1986). The "life history" comes from this range of approaches, and is particularly well suited to the appraisal of practice and career, especially at times of crisis or change. At such moments, it provides both a window on the world and deep insights into the self. It puts the present, crisis or not, into perspective and in context, thereby increasing understanding and perhaps one´s powers of coping. In being concerned with the total life both over time and across all activities (including those other than teaching), it helps to situate current events along a line of development and thus establish a base for the future realistically harnessed to the past. Where current events are at odds with previously held notions of and expectations for career, the life history offers opportunities for reappraisal, suggesting perhaps new permutations and combinations of events and trends, or reawakening old interests and desires temporarily submerged in answer to the exigencies of those times. As well as being instructive, therefore, it can be cathartic and therapeutic.

In a recent research study (Sikes, Measor and Woods, 1985), we used the life history method with some forty teachers. Conversations were held with them, lasting on average for one to one and a half hours, and varying in number from two to seven. The method has been described in detail in Measor (1984) and Woods (1985a). Here, we merely note that our aim was to assist the teachers in reconstructing their past lives - the objective facts, but also, more importantly, their feelings and views at certain times, the influences operating on them, choices made and reasons for them, aspirations and disappointments, changing commitments, relationship between different areas of life, high points and low points, how crises were coped with, major problems overcome and critical periods negotiated, how they adapted to different situations or sought to change situations

The Use of Teacher Biographies

in order to make them more amenable to their own interests. Gradually, over a number of meetings, the life history was built up, rather like a jigsaw in some respects as blank areas were filled in and new aspects recalled. We hoped that our research would provide material that would be helpful to teachers, and others concerned about teacher careers and their implications for education in general; and also contribute towards the theory of teacher careers. Here, we are concerned with pursuing another aspect of the first aim, namely how the approach might be used for self-evaluation and professional development.

The Self Within a Whole Life Framework

We knew from two earlier, linked studies (Woods, 1981, 1984) that life histories might help explain how a teacher might find self-expression in, or give it to, a particular area of the curriculum, and how that self might be perceived to have been built up over the years (see also Goodson, 1980). With "Tom" (the teacher who was the focus of earlier studies) experiences which had contributed to shaping that self were found to be in his early home and parents, in certain teachers and coaches, in books and art, and in his own later family. It was possible to discern wider influences that operated on him - of social class, of religion, of social, political and economic climate; and to trace how these influences and his own interests were mediated by such things as the head teachers he had served under, the reference groups to which he had belonged, and the subject that he had taught. Above all, Tom's life history showed how one teacher over the years "had steered a personal course through various conjunctions of these factors, trying to ensure the predominance of the 'self' co-ordinates, and how the strategies employed in this task have roots deep in his past" (Woods, 1984, p. 260). The life history enabled quite a full appreciation of how this teacher negotiated his way through teaching., engaging with it at a deep personal level and continually juggling commitments and changing situations to maximise his own interests.

163

The advantages of the holistic nature of life histories are evident here in the broadest sense. Smith et al., (1985) p. 184) point to their value in

> ... unravelling threads as intricate as motive structures and personal value systems. For instance, to ask participants to state reasons for undertaking the original task of building Kensington after fifteen years have passed is to invite superficial and self-serving answers. The answers themselves are current word moulds but the original castings may have long since submerged from sight or recall. However, those current moulds are more likely to be interpretable within a life history which dredges up childhood dreams and disappointments. A participant may recall joining the faculty because at that point in her life she was somewhat bored and sought a new challenge while playing down any latent zeal to foster social reform. This same participant might weave a facinating story of a childhood spent righting wrongs, mending birds´ wings and serving as a resident story teller for young children which suggests a more active motive structure than alleviation of boredom.

Such extended, contextualising knowledge is not only gratifying but also constructive, particularly at a time when teachers feel under siege. It can restore their sense of control over their own lives, and help bring out their purposes and integrity. In Tom´s case, he said he had never before thought so intensively and extensively about his earlier life. He found himself "researching" his past between meetings, looking up old letters, documents, photographs, going over old incidents and suddenly remembering new important facts, while he was perhaps cooking a meal, or having a bath. As it came together, therefore, the present self acquired more substantial basis, bits and pieces joined to form new interconnections between the various aspects of his life, and certain patterns of career emerged. In sum, his current self was presented with a wider range of options for future development.

De Weale and Harré (1979, p. 187) sum up the explanatory power of the whole-life perspective, and stress its singularity:

> ... an event can also be made intelligible by locating it in a unique sequential and unfolding process, unique with respect to the individuals involved and perhaps the combination of elements forming its stages as well ... the assisted autobiography is a powerful procedure for generating such an account.

Discovering the Self

Teachers need a catalyst to help them get started on a life history and to construct it. Being involved with our research seemed to provide that for our teachers. They all said they appreciated the chance to reflect on what they had done. There was much mention of routines, and "going and doing things in the same old way without questioning why, or if there might be a better way". The research provided them with an opportuniy to pause awhile from the all-consuming routines, to reflect in depth in response to sympathetic encouragement, and in the process undergo considerable personal change and find new options ahead.

Sally, for example, had rediscovered an identity as artist. On her third visit to her, Pat was greeted with the news that she had "got up an exhibition in the poshest cafe in town" and on the strength of it got some commissions for work. She hadn´t done this for over ten years. She said she had been pushed into thinking about herself and had seen that she was still very much an artist rather than a teacher.

Ray felt that the research helped him to promote a preferred identity. Being involved enabled him to

feel part of an academic community - rather more
than just a teacher. He had just done an M.Ed. and
wanted to get more involved in educational
research. He felt "stuck" in his job. He was not
getting promoted, and the research prevented him
getting bored and stale.

Keith redefined himself out of teaching. He had
been very unhappy in his job. His health suffered,
he got angry very easily with his family and at
times felt suicidal. He told us that reviewing his
experiences had led him to feel he was "just
kidding himself that it might get better". So he
got a job out of teaching and everything, including
his health, improved. Keith had also derived some
therapeutic value from the talks - he said it was
"a bit like having psychoanalysis". There can
indeed be a strong Rogerian line in searching for
the "self that one truly is" and "becoming" that
self or person in the process of re-examining past
experiences. Rogers (1961, p. 122) advocates the
acceptance of self as a

> stream of becoming, not a finished product.
> It means that a person is a fluid process,
> not a fixed and static entity; a flowing
> river of change, not a block of solid
> material; a continually changing
> constellation of potentialities, not a
> fixed quantity of traits.

Typically, teachers got caught up with their own
life story. Several had agreed to only one, or at
the most two meetings. But by the end of the second
they had become so involved that they wanted to
tell more and were asking when we could meet again.
Dave was one of these. He said he liked to
encourage junior staff to talk and reflect on what
they are doing, as he did with us. It gave them a
chance to distance themselves from their work and
analyse what they do. Nobody did it for him these
days.

New Meaning through Life Histories

The life history can add meaning to all teachers'
lives - even if they are retired, or about to
retire. Apart from any personal insights into self,
our older teachers experienced a sense of
fulfilment in making something available to others.
It was their life's work, and pulling it together
in this way and setting it beside others'
experiences might make a contribution, however
small, to general knowledge and improved practice.
Thus Jim told us, "If anything I can say can be of
help to anyone and particularly to those coming up,
then I shall be pleased. I shall feel that it
wasn't all wasted." Jim in fact felt that teaching
was "very selfish because teachers use other people
to gratify themselves ... By talking to you perhaps
I can put something back." So here was an
opportunity for him to pay his dues. He told Pat:

> People need to feel their efforts are
> important. It gives them meaning and
> therefore they try to justify their actions
> as being of significance. People fall apart
> without meaning. You talking to them makes
> them feel important and gives them meaning.

Jim compared the life history to a log/diary he had
to keep in the early days of teaching, and which
was reviewed weekly by the head. He had found this
very useful because it helped to explain certain
things, "why he had been nasty because he had
toothache, etc". He said it helped because it made
you reflect on why you had done what, and you could
use it as a reference point for future practice.

Chris was prompted by Pat's questions to write out
a professional curriculum vitae of what he had done
to date in terms of teaching; for example, projects
he had worked on and how children had responded to
different content and pedagogical approaches. He
was very concerned to communicate effectively,
being aware that he thought and communicated
visually and others did not. He wanted "to get it

right". He also wrote down his philosophy, his aims and intentions. He said that this was going to be very valuable because it gave him a framework for writing his curriculum vitae, which was very useful to him at the time because he was applying for a new job.

Sociology Brought to Life

A systematically studied life history can help inform self-evaluations with new conceptual and theoretical awareness grounded in teacher realities. As Bertaux (1981, p. 31) notes, the life history enables direct access to the level of social relations, which constitute the very substance of sociological "knowledge". John Quicke (1985), in his use of life histories to teach the sociology of education, draws the contrast between some accounts that rather slavishly use sociological concepts to apply to and simply illustrate aspects of their lives in a post-hoc manner, and others who have more successfully internalised them and use them to good effect in making better sense of their lives. He quotes from one, for example, who

> has "discovered" more categories and social
> process in her own experience rather than
> by reference to the literature. For
> instance, the way class cultures are
> transmitted within families and schools via
> the use of siblings as ideal role models,
> and in schools via peers rather than
> teachers ... the way gender issues are
> experienced ... the way social classes
> project their antagonisms on to a common
> enemy ...

There are many examples in our research of "living sociology". Arthur told of his ambition to be an architect, and how his father, who was a coal-miner, was advised by the headmaster that it "cost a lot of money", and "teaching might be better". Arthur felt this was a case of class control. "Being an architect was setting your sights too

The Use of Teacher Biographies

high, and not for the likes of miners' sons'."

From his middle-class viewpoint, John used to go home and tell his parents about the goings-on of the working class pupils in the secondary modern school.

> They didn't believe the things they got up to. It was amazing to me because I'd always done and tried to do what I was told, but these people just didn't seem to care. Doing well at school wasn't important to them. It was a whole new world to me.

Chris, a physics teacher, told how her

> parents couldn't seem to understand that when I came home from university in the holidays I had to work. You were on holiday so why didn't you go out with them and spend time with them. It was hell to get anything done. Study wasn't part of their culture. I was the only one to go to the grammar school and I really used to envy girls who had study bedrooms and everything nice for working. I suppose it was good experience looking back because it makes it easier for me to understand why some of our kids don't do their homework.

There were many illustrations of the influence of gender and a growing awareness of it. Several of the women were told by their fathers that teaching was a suitable career "for a girl". However, the married woman's teaching career took second place to her husband's

> ... and when my husband moved, I moved too. His career was the important one and when I went back to work after the boys went to school I was always able to find a job. At the time it never occurred to me it might be different. Now with all this feminist stuff I might have felt different about it but then it was normal.

169

Even where a woman held a higher status post, she deferred:

> I did want to go on in cancer research but
> my husband had to move. He got promotion
> and I followed him. I suppose at the time I
> could have developed a career - and as you
> say I was working in a university and he
> was a school teacher. I´d never really
> thought about it before, but yes, I did
> have higher status.

An appreciation of how these influences work upon one´s own life is, perhaps, a step towards realising how one might be acting as an agent for them with respect to others. This is not an easy matter. Though there might be plenty of evidence of social class, gender and racial stereotyping in schools, it is difficult for individual teachers to recognise their own part in it. They may genuinely believe that they "treat all children equally" and can present evidence to that effect. Some, however, have very clear awareness of the issue, enlightenment often coming through a consideration of their own personal experiences. Ann, for example, went into some detail about the discussions she organised in her art lessons. These frequently concerned male and female roles within marriage. Ann´s marriage had failed largely because she said her husband "had typical male expectations" and "took her for granted". For her part she had shared his expectations until her children started school and she began to feel a need to "become a person in her own right again, and go back to work." As a result of her own experiences she was determined that her own children and the young people she taught should question stereotypes and she exploited the opportunities her subject offered to encourage them to do so.

One way in which teachers have been successfully encouraged to confront their own practice is through action research. May and Rudduck (1983), for example, have shown how teacher awareness of gender stereotyping can be raised by this means.

The Use of Teacher Biographies

They write,

> Once a group of teachers has become alert
> to the issue of sex-stereotyping, then
> numerous small occurrences suddenly become
> prominent as ´evident´; and as pieces in
> the jigsaw of understanding began to fit
> together, teachers became intrigued: ´I´m
> hooked on this now. I´m fascinated.´

What is important here is not what the teachers
discovered, but that <u>they</u> discovered it, and in
doing so underwent considerable change of attitude.
This, one might argue, is a necessary precondition
for the successful implementation of strategies of
change.

One of the reasons why attitudes are so impervious
to change is because of socialisation in earlier
life into certain frameworks of thought. Judgements
are made from within these, and a lifetime is spent
in consolidating them. What is often helpful here
is, firstly, some sort of cathartic shock to arrest
the routine and provide the motive force for
reconsideration; and, secondly, a lifelong
perspective which enables a tracing back to source
of one´s own attitudes and how they came to be
constituted. The life history provides for both of
these conditions.

The need for grounding conceptual understanding
within life experiences is not to say that
sociological and psychological terms are of no use
to the teacher. Hargreaves (1978) spoke of the
"designatory" capacity of symbolic interactionism.
By this he meant its ability to formulate and
clarify an aspect of life by encapsulating its
pertinent features, giving them a name, and showing
their interrelationships. In this way, teachers´
faceless demons could be identified - the first,
and the essential, step in rendering them harmless.

Mr Court, a retired science teacher, provides an
example of this. He said that reviewing his life
helped him to see his career for what it had been.
He had not realised just how many positive

experiences he had had. Nor had he thought in terms
of analysing it before. Although previously
sceptical about sociology, he had started reading
his wife's sociology textbooks (she was studying
for an A level at night school), and talking more
with her. He liked having his experiences labelled
in scientific terms, and as the sessions with him
progressed he began to employ sociological terms
himself. He said he "had found a new interest".

Group Life Histories

A problem with the life history as a research
method is the tendency to be idiosyncratically
selective and to view the past through the
spectacles worn today. The factors governing such
selection may be various, including the desire to
justify choices and decisions, to rationalise lines
of development as "all for the best", to suppress
personal failures or acute injury, or simply
forgetfulness. There are methods designed to secure
as accurate an account as possible (Dollard, 1935;
Denzin, 1970; Faraday and Plummer, 1979; Goodson,
1980; Bertaux, 1981; Woods, 1985a). However, one of
the best devices for combating these problems is to
situate one's life history in a wider context. This
enables the personal and individual to be seen in
terms of the general and social. Depersonalising
experiences in this way can make them easier to
accept and understand. Thus in our research those
women who forfeited a family life because of the
"laws" concerning married women teachers, those who
looked after aged parents, those whose men were
killed in the wars - all these could feel they
shared something with many others, and that there
was an "honourable" explanation for what they did
and what they had become, and that this had much to
do with the pressure of social forces.

In general terms, people found comfort in the
knowledge that others had had similar experiences,
behaved in similar ways and had had similar
worries. A common remark among our teachers was "I
don't know if what I did was right" or "Other
people might have thought I was wrong." While we
were careful not to pass judgement ourselves in

172

those circumstances, we could point to similar fears and concerns among others, and this sort of information was often greeted with surprise and reassurance.

One such area was that of bad teaching experiences. Chris, for example, said that talking to Pat and hearing what she had to say about older teachers' discipline problems made him feel better, and glad that he had "dared" to confess his to her. A number of teachers telling us about such experiences led to the formulation of the notion of "critical incidents". These were events that were of particular importance for their careers and identities. One particular form occurred during socialisation into the profession, and involved difficulties with pupils. Often the event arose out of challenges by pupils, making new demands on the teacher and calling for a deep search of character. The incidents are "critical" in that they bring to a head a series of events or feelings that may have been building up for some time, and they establish the ground rules for interaction for a considerable time in the future.

A colourful example was that told us by a Glasgwegian woman teacher. One day in 1939 during her probationary year in a tough Glasgow elementary school she entered her balcony classroom to find the boys proudly displaying their genitals on their desks in front of them. She told them to put them away, and frog-marched one of the boys out in such a rush that he fell over the balcony on to the floor some distance below. There was an immediate silence in the classroom, and thereafter she had no more discipline problem.

An incident like this might be recalled by a teacher with horror, and perhaps fright, as well as relief and some pride, perhaps, at the outcome (the boy, it should be noted, had been shaken, but not injured). Most of us experience such moments when events seem to get the better of us and our grip of the situation is called into question. It is comforting to know that this is not peculiar to oneself, that it does not arise solely from personal failings but is a common feature of most teacher´s lives and has a special significance within them. Understanding that some of these "bad" moments act as important change agents and turning points (Strauss, 1959) within a career can bring new confidence that might be shared with those experiencing their own critical incidents. They bring new knowledge of the self, for they highlight and define the crucial elements of demand and resource in unmistakable and pronounced terms, and in a way that demands uncompromising solution. They thus cut through the idealism, the woolliness, the doubt, the generalising, the lack of knowledge that attends the novitiate teacher.

Managing the Teacher Role

Teachers sometimes feel submerged by the role. The demands and pressures are such that a strong element of routine is called for and a set pattern of behaviours found helpful. The problem here is that this assumed role takes on a permanence such as to threaten to turn it into a substantial part of the self. Life histories again provide a shaft of light on the role so as to reveal one´s engagement with it. Our material showed that teachers are not necessarily constrained to act in ways that they feel are contrary to their own natures. Typically teachers negotiate with the role, taking on some aspects to some degree or other - and this can vary in strength and between situations - and rejecting others in a complicated process of dovetailing self and role.

Our teachers seemed to come to recognise this in the course of the discussions. Older teachers, for example, referred to their early days when they were strict and "teacherly" (a) in order to survive, and (b) because being a teacher was novel. Similarly there were phases when people felt they had been more conformist because they wanted promotion. Ann and Pete were prepared to go through the motions of warning pupils about incorrect uniform so that they could say they had. Both of them resented this as they personally did not care about uniform, but Ann would explain to her pupils the hidden meaning of the conformity involved and its relatedness to jobs in later life. Another example of what we termed "strategic compromise" was the way in which many of our art teachers distanced themselves from the teacher role, because it just did not fit in with their ideas about themselves, their lives and their values. They were artists in order to express themselves, but being a teacher for them was not self-expression.

Conclusion

We have heard much about pupil-centredness. In the sense that we have been discussing here, it could be argued that education should also be teacher-centred. Teachers have continually to refine their skills and improve their knowledge. But teaching is not all altruism, and they have, too, to consider their own lives, careers and interests. Especially during a period when the profession as a whole is undergoing profound change, the life history could be a very useful resource in all these respects for a teacher. It aids a principled examinaton of what one of Quicke´s students described as "my favourite subject", i.e. herself, but with discipline rather than indulgence. It can lead to discovery or rediscovery of things about the self, and provide the means by which identity is reconstituted in response to changing circustances. In situating the self within a lifespan in holistic fashion (that is, across all areas of life), it not only anchors the present in the past, but in reassembling the past opens up new options for the future. As it does this, it restores or reaffirms a sense of control over the self as it brings it into focus in unusually detailed analysis, and as it tracks the pursuit of interests through the pressures and constraints that always threaten to frustrate them.

At the same time as the most intimate detail is being recalled from the innermost depths of memory and consciousness there is a "standing back" to appraise it. For the life history encourages the mental discipline necesary for a more distanced, objective viewpoint. This can lead to the identification of new patterns and interconnections and new knowledge at, perhaps, a higher conceptual

175

level. We have also seen how life histories can lead to improved classroom practice for oneself and for others, and how they can have a strong therapeutic effect.

Part of the latter is to do with "talking about it", "getting it off your chest". But speaking about one´s self serves a wider function as one articulates, goes over past incidents, finds the words to describe them and one´s part in them and searches for reasons and explanations. For this is not only one´s own self under examination, but in one´s own terms and language. As Tom put it:

> Now the more we talk about it, the more the uncertain things become, you know, fixed ... I is mine, the minute I put it into words, my words, I´ve got it. Now the only other way is for me to go away and write it all down longhand. When I´ve written it, again it´s mine. So that´s what I believe about this discussion thing. If you don´t write copious notes, if you´re not that sort of person, then you must sit down and talk about it.

Talk thus enlightens, and establishes ownership. But Tom also notes that talking requires an object, a response, and some interaction. Dollard (1935) further points out that life history material does not speak for itself – it has to be interpreted, organised and conceptualised, and the subject may require help to do that. The search for basic material itself requires assistance, in ensuring coverage of areas, specificity of meaning, depth of detail, and contextualising factors (De Waele and Harré, 1979). Ricord (1986) attests to the virtue of subjects having an "open ear" to aid them in reflecting and forming possible dilemma resolutions. Smyth (1982, p. 338) points to the difficulties of the teacher´s job which in itself "may prevent them from accurate self-monitoring". But "to ask them to do it within the framework of clinical supervision, with the aid of a teaching colleague, may be more realistic".

176

The Use of Teacher Biographies

The "aided autobiography", therefore, has much to recommend it in teacher appraisal. The "aid" would appear to be best given by impartial, independent, neutral outsiders, who would appreciate teachers for what they were, taking an interest in them as persons as well as professionals, affording them recognition, acknowledging the importance of their lives in all its myriad and (to some others, perhaps) trivial details, looking on problems, difficulties and weaknesses sympathetically, not judging or attributing blame. It may be difficult for members of one's own staff to meet all these requirements, firstly because they are busy people themselves, and secondly because they might be functionally related to the subject by role, as a "career gatekeeper" perhaps, and thus in a position that required them to exercise judgement.

Our teachers said that they would only talk to other members of staff "if they felt safe with them". As with other methods of ethnographic research, the quality of the product is directly related to the degree of trust generated between the participants. Lack of trust can disguise the undoubted sense of individual need felt by many teachers for this kind of self-enquiry. Ours all said, after the initial ice was broken, that they were very glad to talk about their careers. They found that there was a lot of explaining to do, not only to us but also to themselves. Where sensitively introduced into schools, therefore, the aided life history could make a significant contribution to professional self-development.

REFERENCES

Bertaux, D. (ed.) (1981) Biography and Society: the life history approach in the social sciences, Sage, Beverley Hills.

Denzin, N. (1970) The Research Act in Sociology: a Theoretical Introduction to Sociological Methods, The Butterworth Group Ltd, London.

De Waele, J.-P. & Harré, R. (1979) "Autobiography as a Psychological Method", in Ginsburg, G.P. (ed.) Emerging Strategies in Social Psychological Research, Wiley, London.

Dollard, J. (1935) Criteria for the Life History, Libraries Press, New York.

Dunham, J. (1980) "An Exploratory Comparative Study of Staff Stress in English and German Comprehensive Schools", Educational Review, 32 (1), 11-20.

Faraday, A. & Plummer, K. (1979) "Doing Life Histories", Sociological Review, vol. 27, no. 4.

Goodson, I. (1980) "Life Histories and the Study of Schooling", in Interchange, vol.11, No. 4.

Hargreaves, D.H. (1978) "Whatever Happened to Symbolic Interactionism?" in Barton, L. & Meighan, R.(eds) Sociological Interpretations of Schooling and Classroom: a Reappraisal, 7-22, Nafferton, Driffield

Hughes, E.C. (1937) "Institutional Office and the Person", in Hughes, E.C. (1958) Men and their work, Free Press, New York.

Hustler, D., Cassidy, T. & Coff, T. (1986) Action Research in Classroom and Schools, Allen and Unwin, London.

Kyriacou, C. & Sutcliffe, J. (1979) "Teacher Stress and Satisfaction", Educational Research, 21, 2, 89-96.

May, N. & Rudduck, J. (1983) Sex-Stereotyping and the Early Years of Schooling, The Centre for Applied Research on Eduction, Norwich.

Measor, L. (1984) "Interviewing in Ethnographic Research", in Burgess, R. (ed.) Qualitative Methodology and the Study of Education, Falmer Press, Brighton.

Nixon, J. (1981) A Teacher's Guide to Action Research, Grant McIntyre, London.

Pollard, A. (1985) "Reflective Teaching - the Sociological Contribution", paper given at ESRC Conference on Sociology and the Teacher, St Hilda's College, Oxford.

Quicke, J. (1985) "Using Structured Life Histories to Teach the Sociology of Education", paper given at ESCR Conference on Sociology and the Teacher, St Hilda's College, Oxford.

Ricord, O. (1986) "A Developmental Study of the 'Teaching Self' in Student Teaching", Journal of Education for Teaching, vol. 12, no. 1, 65-76.

Rogers, C. (1961) On Becoming a Person; a therapist's view of psychotherapy, Constable, London.

Roy, W. (1983) Teaching under Attack, Croom Helm, London.

Sikes, P. (1986) The Mid-Career Teacher: Adaptation and Motivation in a Contracting Secondary School System, Unpublished Ph.D. thesis, University of Leeds.

Sikes, P., Measor, L. & Woods, P. (1985) Teacher Careers: Crises and Continuities, Falmer Press, Brighton.

Smith, L.M., Klein, P.R., Dwyer, D.C. & Prunty, J.J. (1985) "Educational Innovators: A Decade and a Half Later", in Ball, S.J. & Goodson, I.F. (eds) Teachers' Lives and Careers, Falmer Press, Brighton.

Smyth, J.A. (1982) "A Teacher Development Approach to Bridging the Practice-Research Gap", Journal of Curriculum Studies, 14, 4, 331-342.

Stenhouse, L. (1975) An Introduction to Curriculum Research and Development, Heinemann, London.

Strauss, A.L. (1959) Mirrors and Masks, The Sociology Press, San Francisco.

Woods, P. (1981) "Strategies, Commitment and Identity: Making and Breaking the Teacher Role", in Barton, L. & Walker, S. (eds) Schools, Teachers and Teaching, Falmer Press, Brighton.

Woods, P. (1984) "Teacher, Self and Curriculum", in Goodson, L.F. & Ball, S.J. (eds) Defining the Curriculum: Histories and Ethnographies, Falmer Press, Barcombe.

Woods, P. (1985a) "Conversations with Teachers", British Educational Research Journal, vol. 11, No. 1, 13-26.

Woods, P. (1985b) "Sociology, Ethnography and Teacher Practice", in Teaching and Teacher Education, vol.1, No. 1. 51-62.

Woods, P. (1986) Inside Schools - The Ethnographic Approach, Routledge and Kegan Paul, London.

8 APPRAISAL OF TEACHER PERFORMANCE

Dr Terence Keen

Most educationalists applaud the decision of ages past to dispose of "payment by results". Today, my daily paper reports another football manager being sacked for the inadequate performance of his team.

Although a supporter of the abolition of payment by results I find it quite amazing that some areas, such as football management, still rely so heavily on second order appraisal of performance. Yet, for me, we, the educationalists, have become too complacent; we must acknowledge the need for appraisal if teaching is to achieve or maintain professional status and effectively educate the clients to the service.

The appraisal debate has raged for many years but by 1990 I remain convinced all teachers will be appraised regularly and routinely. What occupies much of my personal research time is the development of an acceptable mechanism for this appraisal.

When one scans the literature on appraisal in general and teacher appraisal in particular one finds that, almost without exception, the proposals which have been considered rely on behaviourally orientated methodologies akin to the many techniques currently in use in the USA (and in other countries where teaching assessment is common practice). It has been the author's contention that such techniques are an inappropriate way of improving teaching effectiveness in that they demand a pre-specification of criteria deemed to be appropriate, and the teacher is then assessed against this "ideal profile". It is the author's view that the teacher should be perceived as a professional, capable of undertaking his task with autonomy. This is particularly valuable if a mechanism exists to assist him in identifying his strengths and weaknesses so that he can capitalise on the former whilst endeavouring to eradicate the latter (through the application of staff development).

In 1975 the author developed, with Hopwood (Biles, Biles, Keen and Hopwood, 1977), the TARGET system of teacher appraisal. The system reflects Kelly's philosophical position of constructive alternatives (Kelly, 1955), that is to say, an acceptance that an individual's interpretation of the universe is subject to replacement or revision, rather than presenting a static, once-for-all construction of the universe or of any part of it.

The TARGET system utilised repertory grid techniques, allowing a respondent to provide plain language statements to interpret events in terms of discrimination, organisation and the anticipation of future possibilities. Statements of this kind are known as personal constructs, and represent interpretations imposed on events (events associated with teachers and teaching in the case of TARGET) by the respondent. Linkages between constructs illuminate aspects of his construct system, an understanding of which allows speculation concerning his approach to the ordering and anticipation of events.

Over the eleven succeeding years the system was improved and refined in the light of quite extensive field trials as well as further development work. The ready availability of microcomputers in the early 1980s further increased the potential for developing this as a system of self-appraisal determined by means of an interactive conversation with a microcomputer.

The enhanced programming required, well beyond the capabilities of the authors' early programs, was supplied by the research support of Finn Tschudi from the University of Oslo, Norway. The enhanced package, now commercially available from "Tschudi System Sales", Norway, is in increasingly wide use. So what does it do? The system, now called FLEXIGRID (incorporating TARGET), is seen as

182

primarily an interactive system, is non-threatening and non-punitive. It does not rate teachers on a scale between good and bad. And it can be used in complete confidence. Teachers are encouraged to take a microcomputer home with them, and test themselves in complete privacy - with the main intention of identifying their strengths and weaknesses.

The system is based on the principles of personal construct psychology, which, unlike other systems in vogue, does not rely on a behavioural approach. It attempts to raise the perceptual awareness of the teachers and enable them to become more effective in their jobs. The approach enables teachers to understand their behaviour. It makes explicit things they know intuitively to be true but would never be able to tell themselves. So the system is like a mirror which suddenly reveals the teachers as they really are and as people see them. It brings the subconscious to the conscious level.

Appraising oneself is a straightforward procedure. Once one has loaded the basic program into the microcomputer, the teacher then feeds in all the variables which he or she believes relate to an effective or non-effective teacher. Nothing is predetermined.

The variables could range from "badly organised", "involved with audience", "sarcastic", "caring", "good disciplinarian", "bad planner", and "good on preparation", for example.

Once the user has established what the attributes of an effective teacher are - and the deficiencies of a non-effective one - it is possible to compare a variety of known teachers with the "ideal" and also see where one stands in relation to the emergent criteria.

The client/user receives a "printout" which is quite easily interpreted. This consists of a "bar chart" comparing himself or herself against the "most effective" and "most ineffective" teachers known to the client. Firstly one must note that the first indication of effectiveness of teaching is the range or repertoire of skills the teacher has, which can be used in the teaching-learning situation. An indication of this is the number of bars on the chart. Three bars is average with more than 3 indicating above average teaching skills and less than 3 indicating below average skill levels.

Peter, for instance, is average in the example. (see Fig. 1) A detailed manual explains the sophisticated explanation of detail from the printout, but for the purposes of this chapter the

```
PROFILE for: PETER

Definition of ELEMENTS: TYPICAL " MYSELF
                        IDEAL  + JENE ++++
                        WORST  # TONY ####
---------------------------------------------------------------------
                                  Position of ELEMENTS
                          NEGATIVE                POSITIVE
              1              2            3           4           5
NEGATIVE POLE                             .                    POSITIVE POLE
                                          .
COMPONENT 1 ..............................  .         !  ............ COMPONENT 1
                                                     !
thick/weak subj know              ............       !         Academic/bright
off the cuff teacher           ,             ++++++++++++++++++++++++++++++++++ Well prepared
uncaring                         ##############                Caring
Sarcastic                                            !         treat students equal
                                          .          !
COMPONENT 2 ..............................  .  !  ................... COMPONENT 2
                                             !
weak discipline                  ................  .           Good discipline
Lethargic                                 ++++++++++++++++      energetic
                          ##########################
                                          !
COMPONENT 3 ..............................  . !  ................... COMPONENT 3
                                          . !
treat students equal             .................              Sarcastic
Lethargic                                 +++++                 energetic
                          ################
                                          . !
-----------------------------------------------------------------------
                          0    20    40    60    80    100
                               ! MARKS IMPORTANCE OF COMPONENT
-----------------------------------------------------------------------
```

FLEXIGRID v.3.3 September 1986. Copyright (C) Finn Tschudi. University of Oslo. NORWAY
PLOT for data file PETER ##
GRID TITLE: Peter's grid of schoolteachers

FIGURE 1. PETER'S BAR CHART

reader is invited to look at how Peter sees himself
with respect to the best or worst examples of
teachers. It should be clear that he sees himself
as exhibiting some real problems! The words printed
against each bar chart are Peter´s words, used in
the conversation with the computer and selected by
the analysis to best describe each bar on the
chart.

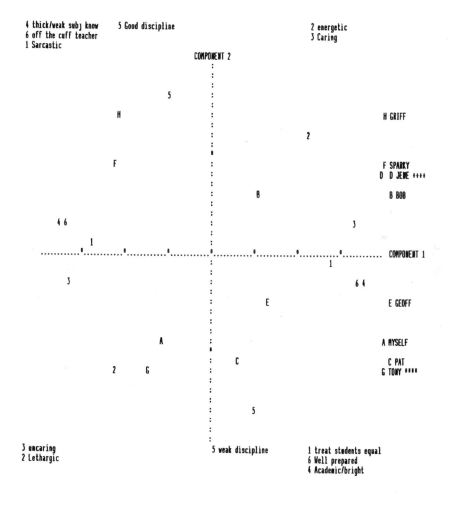

FIGURE 2. PLOT OF PETER'S TWO MAJOR COMPONENTS

The second printout (Fig. 2) is a two-dimensional plot which relates every teacher Peter has considered with every criterion he has used to distinguish between them. The closeness of points (letters for teachers and numbers for descriptions) is an indication of similarity. Thus 6 and 4 are almost coincident so he (Peter) believes "off the cuff teachers" usually have weak subject knowledge. Likewise teachers A (Peter) and G (Tony) are seen as similar (close together) and are best described by 2 (lethargic)!

It is, of course, possible to consider a fuller understanding of the analysis by way of detailed consideration of the statistical analysis of the data elicited in the conversation with the computer. The following section discusses this in a little more detail.

Principles of Interpretation; Individual Consultation

There are different positions as to the role the consultant should play in interpreting the grid. An extreme position is taken by Shaw (1982, p. 352): "It is left to the user to construct his own personal meaning into the results and confirm this directly in terms of the original data." In our experience, however, the client will typically be eager to get help from the consultant, and will ask questions such as: "What does this say about me?", "What does it add up to?" etc. This requires drawing on the consultant´s pre-understanding of the domain under investigation: it is not satisfactory to give non-directive answers since usually the grid does not speak for itself to the client.

In the following we will assume that the person is willing to consider reconstruction and point out some grid features the consultant may look for.

When both SELF and IDEAL SELF are included as elements it may be fruitful to draw attention to possible large discrepancies between these elements. If this occurs and the client confirms that s/he is dissatisfied with her/his position, one may see if there are other elements close to the ideal, or whether elements not included in the grid would have qualities close to the ideal. One may then try to explore with the client whether such an element could be used as a model to emulate, and in this case what behavioural experiments might be performed to try this out. Conversely there may be persons close to the undesired position of SELF, and then one may hypothesise that this is an area of difficulty to work with.

When a specific area is known to be troublesome it will be useful to have that included in the grid, and to explore with the client which other areas are related to this.

The examples above imply that the consultant and the client may try to work out possibilities for movement within the construct space as revealed by the grid. Again principal component analysis provides a clear advantage in that it is easy to visualise "movement". On the other hand reconstruction of the space itself may be called for. In some cases there may be advantages in being at what looks like an undesired position. For our old friend PETER we could for instance ask whether there might be advantages to being SARCASTIC, and conversely whether there might be disadvantages to TREAT STUDENTS EQUAL; similarly for OFF THE CUFF TEACH vs. WELL-PREPARED. This approach may be a fruitful avenue to bring forth new constructs and is described in detail in Tschudi (1977) and Tschudi and Sandsberg (1984).

While obviously not exhaustive, the preceding examples illustrate what may be called a theory-driven approach to grid interpretation. This may be contrasted with a data-driven approach as illustrated in detail by Thomas and Harri-Augstein's (1985) "talk back" where the main emphasis is on having the client comment systematically on all the clusters in FOCUS. Notice here that this approach may be improved by paying attention to Z-scores whch will invite emphasising the most significant clusters. This approach seems particularly appropriate when grids are being used in what Stewart and Stewart (1981, p. 92-3) call an "extractive sense". In this case the client is a recognised expert in some field (for instance, teaching) and the point is to make her/his knowledge as explicit as possible in order to provide clearer standards (e.g., for training others) or as a step in building an expert system. Obviously the consultant´s pre-understanding may play a minor role in such cases. What I here call a theory-driven approach corresponds to Stewart and Stewart´s conception of using grids in a "semi-counselling sense" where the point is to feed grid results back to help the client "overcome any obstacles", and we emphasise that in such cases extensive pre-understanding is required for the consultant.

Any discussion of grid interpretation must be incomplete if we do not consider the relation between the consultant and the client. In the traditional study of concepts it is now becoming evident that features in no way are "given" as firmly attached to objects, but strongly depend upon the particular "theory of the world" or background context brought forth. This is convincingly argued by Murphy and Medin (1985). Trzebinski (1985) illustrates by grid methodology how "implicit personality theory" depends upon goal structure (context), and argues against any fixed conception of there being but one such theory. On one level this underscores the importance of having a definite purpose for doing a grid (see, for instance, Shaw, 1980).

Taking the general argument above one level further, it follows that the relation between consultant and client may be very important for how the grid results will be construed. Features do not reside in objects and similarly the implications of a grid do not reside in the analysis of the grid (whatever the mathematical sophistication of the analysis may be) but emerge from a human interaction. Consequently it is very important that the atmosphere is productive, characterised by openness, trust and co-operation. This, of course, would also follow from a Rogerian position. From our Kellian perspective we emphasise seeing grid interpretation as a dialogue where the consultant must be able to play a role in the Kellian sense with the client. (See Tschudi and Rommetveit, 1982, for further discussion of dialogue in the context of Kelly´s Sociality Corollary.)

An important property of such a dialogue is that new ideas may emerge. This again underscores that any list of features of what to look for in grids must necessarily be incomplete. Another way to make this point is to note that, when the aim is to help the client to bring forth new constructions, the consultant must be able to serve as a model!

A characteristic of the FLEXIGRID package is that it invites interpreting grid structures on different levels. We have suggested starting interpretations with the most striking or obvious features of the displays, whether these are TARGET profiles, the more elaborate PCA plot(s), or combinations of the above displays. The main impact of such displays may well be that they provide an external point of reference which may serve as an important aid to reconstruction (a variety of quite different displays may also be valuable from this point of view).

Sometimes quite obvious features of the grid display may be sufficient to answer the substantive questions which led to the grid being elicited in the first place. In such cases there is little reason to delve further into all the extra statistical information provided by FLEXIGRID. It is, however, important that the consultant gets thoroughly acquainted with the package by analysing several grids all with different methods in order to acquire familiarity with what really is "obvious". Here a close study of residuals and goodness of fit information is essential.

Typically, however, the consultant may want to look into the finer grain of the grid structure either because the obvious features were well-known beforehand or for other reasons. A problem may then arise in that the raw data and what the display suggests can point in different directions.

A more overriding criterion might be whether separate hypotheses, from a grid fit into some larger coherent pattern. Perhaps grid interpretation should not so much be seen as an exercise in multivariate methods (as often seems to be the case), but as a hermeneutical endeavour. Kelly´s (1955) analysis of self-characterisation may serve as a model of how separate bits of information may be welded together.

To return to our theme of dialogue: this information should be used judiciously. We have pointed out that a computer may be facilitative or inhibitive in elicitation. The same holds for statistical information in interpretation. In some cases it may be useful for the client in sharpening the salient aspects of the mirror the grid provides or together with the consultant to sort out different hypotheses, but too much focus on this information may in many cases be distractive. It is the responsibility of the consultant to decide to what extent and with what level of mathematical sophistication to share this information with the client although obviously this will depend upon the relation between the client and the consultant and the background of the client.

One should never forget that the superordinate goal should be to clarify existing structure or to provide help to reconstrue. All displays and accompanying statistical information should be seen as means to this end, never as an end in itself.

Definite reconstruction will rarely take place in the context of a dialogue centred on understanding the grid results. But it should lead to plans of action, "behavioural experiments" to use the Kellian expression, and the results of these experiments should later be evaluated. Again grid methods may be useful, typically with partly different elements and constructs. The ideal situation would be where the consultant is able to make specific hypotheses as to how the grid structure will change to test her/his understanding of the client's world.

Using FLEXIGRID should be seen as a computer assisted procedure. The computer is no panacea, but judiciously used it may be an important aid to the consultant and the client. The printout can, at one level, be interpreted by the teacher himself or herself, or can form the basis of detailed staff development in conjunction with a specialist. For most teachers the "do it yourself" approach generated excellent results!

The author is therefore postulating a model which does not appraise teachers against pre-determined criteria, but instead assists them to identify their own strengths and weaknesses on criteria they, as professionals, see as relevant and important.

Critics of this approach argue that, if no one has told teachers what is good or bad, then they could easily be working entirely on the wrong lines. This is, however, not the point. From the author's perspective the task is to help teachers as professional people identify their own strengths and weaknesses, and not to impose some kind of outside model of what is or is not competence. Thus the system varies from most appraisal techniques developed in other countries, which have been based on a behavioural approach. Basically these have looked at good practice and drawn up a check list. The problem is that when one applies the checklist one is making assumptions that what is effective with one group of students will work with another, and this is just not true.

In the 1985 White Paper "Better Schools" Sir Keith Joseph indicated that legislation on appraisal was not just a gleam in the eye of those who would wish to see it imposed on the teaching profession.

The White Paper said:

> It is propsed therefore that the Secretary of State's existing powers for regulating the employment of teachers should be

extended to enable him in appropriate
circumstances to require local education
authorities to appraise the performance of
their teachers. (DES, 1985)

Appraisal will come - let's ensure it comes in a
way we - the educationalists - recognise as valid
and reliable, not, as the author fears may be the
case, in the form of a checklist of largely
irrelevant criteria. Such a scheme, whilst being a
long way from "payment by results", would be no
more realistic than firing of football managers for
the lack of success of their team!

BIBLIOGRAPHY AND REFERENCES

Aagaard, L.E. (1985) Kelliansk teori og metode som hjelpemiddel for organisasjonsklinikerm i hans arbeid med mennesker i funksjonelle grupper, Unpublished Master's thesis. (Kellian theory and method as an aid for the organisational clinician in his work with people in functional groups.) University of Oslo, Oslo, Norway.

Adams-Webber, J.R. (1979) Personal Construct Theory. Concepts and Applications, Wiley, New York.

Bell, R.C. & Keen, T.R. (1980) "A statistical aid for the grid administrator", International Journal of Man Machine Studies, 13, 143-150.

Biles, B., Biles, M., Keen, T. & Hopwood, W. (1977) Unpublished paper. Presented at the International Conference on the Improvement of University Teaching, Newcastle.

Chiari, G., Mancini, F., Nicolo, F. & Nuzzo, M.L. (1985) "The hierarchical construct systems in terms of the range of convenience: a model", paper presented at the VIIth International Personal Construct Psychology Congress, Cambridge, England.

Crocket, W.H. (1982) "The organisation of construct systems: the organizaton corollary", in J.C. Mancuso & J.R. Adams-Webber (eds), The Construing Person, 62-95. Praeger, New York.

DES (1985) Better Schools, HMSO, London.

Drayfus, H.L. (1979) What computers can't do, (revised edn.), Harper and Row, New York.

Drayfus, H. L. (1985) "Competent Systems: the limits of calculative rationality". unpublished manuscript.

Eckblad, G. (1980) "The Curvex: simple order structure revealed in ratings of complexity, interestingness, and pleasantness", Scandinavian Journal of Psychology, 21, 1-16.

Eckblad, G. (1981) Scheme theory. A conceptual framework for cognitive motivation processes, Academic Press, London.

Feigenbaum, E. & McCurdock, P. (1983) The fifth generation: artificial intelligence and Japan's computer challenge to the world, Addison-Wesley, New York.

Fransella, F. & Bannister, D. (1977) A Manual for
Repertory Grid Technique, Academic Press,
New York.

Gadamer, H.G. (1960) Truth and Method, Cambridge
University Press, Cambridge.

Higginbotham, P. & Bannister, D. (1982) "The GAB
computer program for the analysis of repertory
grid data", University of Leeds.

Johnson, S.C. (1968) A Simple Cluster Statistic,
Mimeographed report, Bell Telephone Laboratories,
Murray Hill, New Jersey.

Keen, T.R. (1979) "TARGET: Two years on", paper
presented at the Third International Personal
Construct Psychology Congress, Utrecht,
Netherlands.

Keen, T.R. & Bell, R.C. (1980) "One thing leads to
another: a new approach to elicitation in
repertory grid technique", International Journal
of Man-Machine Studies, 13, 81-85.

Kelly, G.A. (1955) The Psychology of Personal
Constructs, Norton, New York.

Leach, C. (1981) "Direct analysis of a repertory
grid", in M.L.G. Shaw (ed.) Recent advances in
personal construct technology, pp. 217-232,
Academic Press, London.

Mancuso, J.C. & Eimer, B.N. (1982) "Fitting things
into sorts: the range corollary", in J.C.
Mancuso & J.R. Adams-Webber (eds) The Construing
Person, pp. 130-151, Praeger, New York.

Mendoza, S. (1985) "The exchange grid", in N. Beail
(ed.) Repertory Grid Technique and Personal
Constructs, pp. 173-189, Croom Helm, London.

Miller, G.A. (1967) "Psycholinguistic approaches to
the study of communication", in D.L. Arm (ed.)
Journey in Science: small steps - great
strides, pp. 22-73, The University of New Mexico
Press, Albuquerque.

Miller, G.A. (1969) "A psychological method to
investigate verbal concepts", Journal of
Mathematical Psychology, 6, 169-191.

Murphy, G.L. & Medin, D.L. (1985) "The role of
theories in conceptual coherence", Psychological
Review, 92, 289-316.

Pope, M.L. & Keen, T.R. (1981) Personal Construct
Psychology and Education, Academic Press, London.

Ryle, A. (1975) Frames and Cages, Sussex University
Press, London.

Ryle, A. (1985) "The Dyad grid and psychotherapy research", in N. Beail (ed.) Repertory Grid Technique and Personal Constructs, pp. 190-206, Croom Helm, London.

Shaw, M.L.G. (1980) On Becoming a Personal Scientist, Academic Press, London.

Shaw, M.L.G. (1982) "PLANET: some experiences in creating an integrated system for repertory grid applications on a microcomputer", International Journal of Man-Machine Studies, 17, 345-360.

Shaw, M.L.G. & Gaines, B.R. (1981) "The personal computer and the personal scientist", paper presented at the British Computer Society conference, Institute of Education, London.

Shaw, M.L.G. & Thomas, L.F. (1978) "FOCUS on education - an interactive computer system for the development and analysis of repertory grids", International Journal of Man-Machine Studies, 10, 138-173.

Slater, P. (1976) Exploration of Intrapersonal Space, vol. 1, Wiley, London.

Sneath, P.H.A. & Sokal, R.R. (1973) Numerical Taxonomy, Freeman, San Francisco.

Stewart, V. & Stewart, A. (1981) Business Applications of Repertory Grid, McGraw-Hill, London.

Thomas, L.F. & Harri-Augstein, E.S. (1985) Self-organised Learning. Foundations of a Conversational Science for Psychology , Routledge & Kegan Paul, London.

Trzebinski, J. (1985) "Action oriented representatons of implicit personality theories", Journal of Personality and Social Psychology, 48, 1266-1278.

Tschudi, F. (1972) The latent, the manifest and the recontructed in multivariate data reduction models, Unpublished doctoral dissertation, University of Oslo, Oslo.

Tschudi, F. (1977) "Loaded and honest questions. A construct theory view of symptoms and therapy", in D. Bannister (ed.) New Perspectives in Personal Construct Theory, pp. 326-349, Academic Press, London.

Tschudi, F. (1984) Operating Manual for: FLEXIGRID version 2.1. August 1984, University of Oslo, Oslo.

Tschudi, F. (1985) FLEXIGRID version 3.1. April 1985. Supplementary Manual, University of Oslo, Oslo.

Tschudi, F. & Rommetveit, R. (1982) "Sociality, intersubjectivity, and social processes", in J.C. Mancuso & J.R. Adams-Webber (eds) The Construing Person, pp. 235-261, Praeger, New York.

Tschudi, F. & Sandsberg, S. (1984) "On the advantage of symptoms: exploring the client's construing", Scandinavian Journal of Psychology, 25, 169-177.

Turkel, S. (1984) The Second Self. Computers and the human spirit, Simon & Schuster, New York.

Weizenbaum, J. (1976) Computer Power and Human Reason. From judgement to calculation, Freeman, San Francisco.

9 LEARNER–CENTRED LEARNING FOR PROFESSIONAL DEVELOPMENT

John Cowan and Anna Garry

Learner-Centred Learning

We picture our readership as including many who are not engaged in full-time educational work, and are unfamiliar with recent educational literature. We hope to describe what we have been doing without using specialised terms that will make the readers reach for their educational dictionaries, or a more readable text. And so without further ado we want to dispose of any complications implicit in our title by explaining what "learner-centred learning" meant to us in our CPD work.

We tried to identify the needs of each learner so that appropriate aims could be formulated. We created circumstances in which the learners were able to follow methods of study which were convenient and effective for them, and which took proper cognisance of the knowledge and understanding which they already possessed.

We set out to place the direction of the process of learning and development in the hands of the learner, as far as that was possible. We arranged to supply information and explanations, especially where they were needed or requested. We also took an initiative on occasions by posing questions presenting challenges and highlighting inconsistencies. We saw ourselves as helping along the process of learning and development, which can more shortly be described as "facilitation"; and we hope you won't mind if we continue to use that word from now on.

We set out to cater for learners who would be in contact with a facilitator who would support their learning and arrange a programme of events which would stimulate and encourage the learners to make progress. That's the type of scheme we were trying to create when we set out on our project in 1984 (Cowan and Garry, 1986a). It is that approach which we will describe in the remainder of this chapter - and which we will call "learner-centred learning".

How does this Approach Compare with the Status Quo?

The philosophy which we will advocate in this chapter, and which we have tried to implement in our pilot scheme, is as different (Cowan, 1986) from the conventional type of CPD course as a family home is from a motel bedroom.

Our approach seeks to identify the total pattern of needs as seen by the individuals concerned, and sets out to offer an adequate response to them; the status quo selects a restricted number of aims and objectives and markets a standard course, on a take it or leave it basis, to customers who declare an interest in these goals.

By focusing on aims which have been identified by the participants as important, our course is assured of commitment (provided the facilitation is effective); the drop-out rates from conventional courses tell a different story.

Development programmes which concentrate on active learning and interaction between engineers lead to immediate learning and development of a meaningful and worthwhile kind; a conventional course, which provides didactic instruction and a set of lecture notes, leads to relatively little retention of understanding without subsequent effort - and seldom makes any attempt to cater for higher level aims.

We cannot see any real comparison between the two types of approach. The isolated "taught" course has a place in continuing professional development - but that place is surely as a component within a learner-centred programme devised to respond to the total pattern of needs for an individual, insofar as these can be ascertained.

Why did we Decide to Approach CPD in This Way?

Worthwhile learning and development takes place when new items are linked onto items of established understanding with which such linkages will be meaningful; the more meaningful the linkages, the firmer the grasp of the new idea — and the more difficult it is for it to be forgotten. Prior learning, then, influences subsequent learning.

In any activity which we might plan and run, we anticipated that we would have to deal with a great variety of prior learning. Even if all the participants were also at roughly the same stage in their professional development, it was virtually inevitable that their prior experiences in engineering would differ. Hence it was essential for us to find ways to recognise and cater for the individuality of the prior learning which our participants would bring to any activity which we planned for them.

Equally important to the facilitator is individuality with regard to favoured learning styles. One participant may lack the ability for self-appraisal and for logic and well-ordered thinking; the next, otherwise similar to the first, seems to have a well-developed ability to define the salient features of a problem and establish useful criteria, but may lack creativity in generating the solutions or the strategies through which to obtain a solution. The needs of two such participants are clearly <u>totally</u> different despite marked similarity in their eventual goals and in their prior experience.

Individuality of needs and individuality of prior learning should, we believe, influence how development takes place, <u>and</u> how it is facilitated.

Why do we Argue so Strongly for This Approach?

Our belief in the importance of the individual in professional development owes much to our own personal experiences of professional development.

We have frequently been intensely frustrated by professional development activities which assumed knowledge or experience which we did not possess, or which disregarded the experience which we <u>did</u> have - and thus wasted endless time going over <u>old</u> ground. We have been even more frustrated by activities which followed a predetermined programme and took no cognisance of our needs, interests and concerns - many of which have even been generated by the earlier parts of the programme. We have often been annoyed when we received no assistance with relating the isolated segments of learning in the course to our professional lives.

Most of all, perhaps, we have resented CPD activities which presented information in unhelpful ways - as far as we were concerned; or forced us to follow programmes which did not allow us time to think through important issues; or which did not help us to find the full answers to the questions which concerned us. They seemed to take no notice of our needs - as learners.

Consequently we have now taken charge of our own development. We build on the learning we already possess; we identify our needs and we find ways of satisfying them; we work in our own ways and monitor our own progress - with, we hope, a healthy awareness of what is available elsewhere.

To be honest, we must admit that we believe in the type of approach we are advocating because it is the only one we have found which has worked for us. It is only recently that we have learned to make it appear a respectable and objective choice by justifying it in terms of what the psychologists and educationists write about the process of learning and development.

Were the Needs as Varied as we Expected?

In a group of mature candidates seeking chartered status by writing an original 10,000 word report (rather like a short thesis) we helped individuals to identify needs concerned with fundamental text book instruction, communication skills, computation, library searching, analysis of data and formulation of criteria. Amongst young engineers preparing for a professional interview we encountered diverse needs covering ability to engage in unprepared dialogue, mastery of legal principles, ability to formulate arguments logically and rectifying stark omissions in education and training.

Our workshops therefore began from identification of needs and progressed to offering responses to appropriate groups or sub-groups, under the types of heading we have quoted.

How Did We Begin?

We were fortunate because we began in what was almost an intellectual vacuum. We didn't know very much about our prospective participants; we had only a vague impression of what their needs might be; and we could not commit ourselves to even the vaguest of outlines for training events.

So we began at the beginning. We spent considerable time meeting potential participants individually. We asked many questions, finding out all that we could about their needs; and we lent willing ears to the competence which they wished to display to us. We also discussed with them, to some extent, the ways in which they liked to work and learn. And so, gradually, we moved towards a position in which we were ready to take the first steps in offering meaningful facilitation to each individual interviewee.

Then it was time to think in terms of groups of participants. We created programmes in which, by using interactions between participants, we could coax a group to follow through the steps which we had taken with each of our individual interviewees. Where we had seen a pattern of similarity amidst the individuals whom we had interviewed, we anticipated that this similarity might be found amongst the majority of our workshop participants;

where we had encountered marked individuality, we tried to work our programme details which would cater for that type of individual need or response, if it arose.

We intended to be flexible in our use of our plans. Every group could be different from its predecessors, or from our expectations. At any moment needs might emerge which would be important - but unpredicted. Prior learning might be presented and could be shared or utilised within the group - or, against all expectations, it might be absent, with the result that immediate remedial action would be needed and should be arranged. The programme should always be responsive.

We can all profit from experience, but at the same time we can become hidebound if we rely too much on what we did (successfully) in the past.

What are the Main Features of This Type of Programme?

1. We start by identifying needs and prior experience, because these are the basis on which development will be built. We <u>expect</u> our participants to be different; therefore we (and they) must find out what the significant differences are.

2. We then create one or two experiences within which participants can discover or explore other needs, of which they are unaware - or which they were unwilling to declare in strange company.

3. We also make space for "talking time", in which participants establish credibility for themselves in the eyes of their peers, and of the facilitator.

4. We anticipate that many of our participants will look to us for motivation or to strengthen their confidence in themselves.

5. We try to respond to some of the
expressed needs, with an early input of
information which will be useful and
valued. This should lead directly to
activity centred on tasks.

We design and present tasks which will
prompt individuals to develop in their own
ways.

6. We plan to develop meaningful
relationships. In a situation where many of
the aims are affective rather than
cognitive, values are transferred across
meaningful bridges of interrelationships
between people who respect each other.
These bridges must be created before they
can be used.

7. We plan our activities so each
participant can emerge as a real person -
not just because we value people or because
they are more comfortable that way, but
because many of their needs will be highly
personal ones which will only emerge when
the participants see that they are in a
situation where they are respected as the
people who they are.

8. We arrange to facilitate an activity
which will lead to self-appraisal near the
end of the programme. Participants may then
identify for themselves (or for their
peers) further needs - which we can cover
before the programme finishes.

9. If the participants seek formal
recognition for the development they are
undertaking (as in obtaining chartered
status), it is vital for us to be <u>extremely</u>
well prepared to answer a wide variety of
highly detailed questions about the
requirements and the procedures through
which these requirements are satisfied.

203

10. We take the initiative in setting up
arrangements for significant collaboration
between participants in "self-help" groups.

11. The style of working, although
individualised, should expedite the process
of learning and development by harnessing
interactions between peers, or between
participants and the senior members of the
profession.

What is Our Function in This Approach?

The prime role for staff in activities of this type
is to facilitate learning – in many ways, and in
many different situations (Garry, 1983). We have
found Carl Rogers (1983) helpful in offering us
advice which relates to that situation. He expounds
a powerful philosophy in everyday terms, helping us
to work out our own solutions to problems which he
has not covered.

In our experience the facilitator must sometimes

- question (without implying the answer)

- mirror (to make it clearer to the participants
what they are doing)

- act as a conscience (reminding participants of
criteria or aims)

- provide structure (to avoid wasted time in
unproductive group dynamics)

There are, however, many different facets of the
role, which cannot be summarised in a few lines. We
did our best in a 90-page project handbook – but
even that was just a beginning (Cowan and Garry,
1986b)!

It is temptingly easy for traditionally educated

teachers to slip into the didactic mode, telling learners what they should know and how they should apply that knowledge. Yet no learner will develop cognitive ability without forging it out personally, and relating it (in some form of active learning situation) to prior understanding and experience. So for that reason facilitation is more desirable than instruction - except for lower level aims - <u>and</u> more difficult!

Alan Harding, a master of facilitation, read the (almost) final draft of this chapter and commented:

> A key function in facilitation is the facilitation of need identification and acceptance. The learning can in many ways be self conducted. The perception and acceptance of many needs may demand facilitation.
>
> This very important aspect of facilitation should be highlighted.

We would not wish to add to that important comment.

How did we Design Workshop Outlines?

We found little assistance in the literature - so we were virtually on our own.

We had four main ways of developing workshop outlines:

1) working from the objectives

2) using a scheme that worked elsewhere

3) working outwards from a central activity

4) exploring the seed of an idea.

Recently we produced a list of possible approaches

(Cowan & Garry, 1986b), rather like the one above - and proceeded to expand on it, in what we hoped was a rational and helpful way. Looking back on what we wrote, we now feel that it looks too methodical and reassuring. It doesn't convey the excitement and the frustration, the trials and the errors - and above all the essential creativeness of what we have experienced in workshop design. So we will not attempt to provide you with recipes which you can follow step by step, in the expectation that mere procedures will lead you to a satisfactory outcome. Instead we prefer to attempt to convey something of the flavour of how we have experienced that part of our job.

How do we Design Workshop Activities?

Workshop design, for us, begins with a large and symbolically empty sheet of paper on a flip chart stand. One of us takes the initiative to be the scribe; the other has a pen of a different colour and adds suplementary notes as we go along.

We always begin by chewing over what it is that we hope this activity will do for our participants. What will they learn which they didn't know before? What will they analyse and explore - perhaps by trying to apply it and then evaluating that experience? What abilities will they develop or scrutinise so that they will perform more effectively next time?

The beginning of good design, for us, is rooted in informal discussion of our assorted answers to that question; for these now express our goals as the facilitators of this particular event. They also hint at the features which we must incorporate in our solutions, if we wish to create appropriate conditions for learning.

The easiest way to design a workshop occurs for us when our detailed discussion of the objectives has put them into a logical and developing order, describing what the participants should do or should be able to do better. This sequence can virtually become a skeleton programme for the activity. It only remains for us to work out ways of presenting the various tasks so that we do not presume what the learners will learn (or how they will learn) but merely stipulate desirable experiences and a potentially effective programme structure.

That's all fairly easy, and temptingly straightforward. Unfortunately this approach to design can easily end up with a logical, methodical and somewhat insipidly boring programme, which can't be fundamentally changed by grafting on gimmicks or novelties in the hope of boosting the motivation of the participants.

The worst way to design a workshop, in our experience, is to have an idea already before we start. It may be something that we've done before with a similar group, or a programme which someone else used, which we admired. In these circumstances we are saddled with a framework which has already been virtually finalised, whether we admit that to ourselves or not. The process of design is really only a matter of adaptation in which we modify the scheme to try to make it fit the objectives which we have on this occasion, and the target group with whom we expect to be working. The possibilities are constrained by the chosen outline - and many other options are not explored.

This approach does not call for imagination or creative talent; it merely requires an ability to recognise and remember useful outlines, and a readiness to introduce modifications to fit a particular situation. We have not found it a fruitful way to design. That could either be because we like to indulge ourselves in the excitement of design, or because we are poor plagiarists.

The most creative method of workshop design (for us) begins from the nucleus of a single activity.

We regard a workshop as being composed of a number of "activities" which are linked together to form the total programme. Usually an activity finishes when the participants produce something - a tangible output in one form or another. That output is then used in the following (or a subsequent) activity.

In a well-designed workshop the key activity in the chain should be educationally compatible with the central goal of the workshop. That's why, in the most creative design, we find it good to start at the heart of the event, concentrating on the real challenge implicit in the goals we have chosen and explored in the opening stages. Having analysed our aspirations and constraints, we design a response which genuinely reacts to all the components we have identified in our analysis.

We find that our exploratory discussion, if it is properly carried out, implies "advice" which in turn suggests to us the features which should be present in this central activity. If we are sufficiently attentive to our analysis, we find that we can accumulate a collection of pieces of advice and weld them together into a truly creative and satisfying response to our brief.

Nevertheless a feasible outline doesn't emerge in a moment, nor does it usually happen that we get a reasonable scheme first time round. Once we have our central idea, we then have to work out how to reach that part of our programme by constructing a sequence of activities which will precede the central one; we also have to move on through the sequence to a potentially successful conclusion, which means thinking out the subsequent activities which will consolidate the learning and make good any omissions, deficiencies or areas of misunderstanding.

We now probably have a number of flip chart sheets bluetacked around the walls. Our rough outline is hidden there, somewhere, in a variety of handwritings and inks. So it is time for us to double back, and check the outline from beginning to end. We must find the places where the pieces in the jigsaw do not fit together neatly - and also the aspects of our suggestions which are likely to introduce difficulties for facilitators or participants.

Occasionally this iterative part of creative
design, in which the outline may again change,
calls for a new sheet - and a new statement. More
commonly, however, the final draft scheme emerges
phoenix-like from the debris (if not the ashes) of
its predecessors, with an annotation (perhaps in
the thickest and blackest of pens) to indicate
what, if anything, of the first suggestions has
been retained.

The workshops with which we have been most
satisfied have been designed in this interactive
way.

The most uncertain way to design a workshop is
very similar to the one we have just described,
except that it begins from an apparently more
hopeless situation.

There are times when we find it difficult to
produce a coherent and credible list of objectives,
because we´re not quite sure how to describe our
aspirations for the participants in behavioural
terms. Sometimes we just cannot picture a central
activity which could be the crucible for the
learning and development which should take place.
On these occasions we may have no more than a germ
of an idea to work on. This could arise perhaps
from an experience which was formative for us, or
could be an almost crazy notion which keeps coming
into our minds, because nothing else is there to
take up our attention.

When we have nothing more definite to go on, we
literally play around with our vague idea, to see
what might be linked to it and to discover if it
could have anything to offer us. This means that we
must juggle with two streams of thought at the same
time, on these increasingly confused flip chart
sheets. One set concerns the development of an
activity which should be useful, motivating and
challenging for the participants; the other set
relate's to our aims and objectives, which - you
will remember - were not yet properly formulated,
and are still as much in a state of flux as is the
development of our programme.

After spending a reasonable amount of time in almost aimless exploration, we are sometimes in a position to draft a tentative list of objectives and associate them with rough suggestions for a starting activity. We have then reached a situation corresponding to the starting point in the last strategy we described. (The "worst" way!)

Whatever approach we use, we go round and round, refining our scheme in a number of iterative cycles. For we must make sure that the participants will have ample opportunity to learn and develop by exploring, analysing, focusing on process - and just by doing.

We look at the entire event from the participants' viewpoint, and anticipate their feelings at each stage. We check that there will be stimulating challenges and tasks to encourage the involvement of all or most of the participants in a group. We also make sure that the challenges are not likely to intimidate.

Finally, we examine the outline step by step, looking for problems and snags in respect of timing, arrangements, inadequate explanation of tasks and so on.

Were We Successful?

Our remit was to find out if self-help groups, following the type of approach we have been describing, could usefully be set up and supported in the workplace as an agency to promote professional development.

Much of our time was devoted to formative evaluation - of the programme outlines, of the presentation styles which we used, and of the responses which we gave to individuals both orally and in writing. It was "evaluation" because data and information about what had happened were gathered, analysed and compared with predetermined criteria for the activity. It was "formative" because our object was not to make judgements of

the effectiveness of the event, but to identify
scope for (and means of) effecting improvement.

Our project led us to conclude that learner-centred
learning is essential as far as continuing
professional development is concerned. We are never
able to compare like with like; and we doubt if
that would ever be possible, for the aims of
learner-centred learning are inevitably wider than
those of any of the conventional examples of CPD
with which we are familiar. So we cannot make a
direct comparison or an (absolute) summative
evaluation. And we did not initially progress as
rapidly as we had hoped in establishing self-help
groups.

We have, of course, interviewed many of our
participants. We asked them all to complete a
questionnaire - from which it emerged that a large
majority were pleased with what they had been
offered and found the programme helpful, supportive
and encouraging. We can point to relatively high
success rates (for our admittedly small groups) in
the professional examinations for which some chose
to prepare themselves, and to the tangible progress
which several have already made in studying for
part-time degrees which would previously have
appeared to be totally out of the question as a
possibility. That is really our only evaluation of
the end result. We have no shame in making that
admission, bcause we feel that the purpose of a
feasibility study is to establish feasibility of a
prototype, and not to produce or evaluate a
"production model".

What Were Our Main Problems?

Naturally we would like to think that most of our
difficulties reflected the intrinsic difficulty of
this approach to continuing professional education,
and our roles within it. Our main problems were
that:

> It is much more difficult to facilitate
> than to teach.

Very little specific advice is available
about how to plan and run workshop
activities which will involve
active learning and respond to particular
and total declarations of needs.

Participants find that it is threatening to
be asked to take charge of their own
learning and development; they tend to look
for ways to evade that necessary challenge
and responsibility.

There is often confusion in active learning
between providing an opportunity for
participants to practice, and creating
situations in which their ability will be
enhanced.

It is intrinsically difficult to devise
group situations in which participants will
behave effectively as individuals without
receiving the personal (and uneconomical)
attention of a facilitator on a one-to-one
basis.

Those who are engaged in engineering
education have paid regrettably little
attention to achieving affective aims,   or
to sustaining (and building up) morale.

Participants often do not recognise all of
their needs, will resent a diagnosis of
needs by a third party and - most important
of all - will not accept and respond to
that need unless they diagnose it for
themselves.

Did We Identify All the Performance-Related Needs?

At a given point in time the needs of an individual
for continuing professional development can be
divided into those which the subject is capable of
formulating and expressing in terms which would be
comprehensible to someone else, and those which the
subject cannot formulate. Formulation   may   be

impossible either because (s)he is unaware of their existence or because a nagging feeling of want is not yet sufficiently tangible to be expressed as needs.

The formulated needs, in their turn, can again be subdivided. In a given subject there are some which the subject is willing to declare or express - and some which the subject prefers not to expose, for one reason or another. If the environment is supportive and the subject trusts the assembled company, then the proportion of formulated needs which (s)he is willing to express becomes much greater. If on the other hand the company is threatening, and the subject is concerned about the consequences of exposing needs which also define weaknesses, then the proportion of expressible needs decreases.

As facilitators we try to make it possible, through interactions, for learners to formulate a proportion of those vaguely appreciated needs which, for a given individual, lie near the border-line between formulated and unformulated. We can also strive to establish the type of environment within a workshop group which will optimise the proportion of formulated needs which will be expressed.

It is extremely unlikely that all formulated needs will ever be expressed, except to very close friends; and it is certain that many unformulated needs cannot be determined in the short term from the subjects, and may not even be ascertained from other sources. That is why it would never be possible to identify all the performance-related needs, in our opinion.

Are Performance-Related Issues Capable of Educational Intervention?

We cannot <u>direct</u> development within the style of continuing professional education which we have tried to describe here. We can only facilitate it - and support any initiatives which the participants determine, and to which they make a commitment. The direction of development, the values on which it is based, the extent of commitment to it and the meaningful evaluation of that personal development against personally selected criteria, must all lie with the person concerned - if the development is to be deep and meaningful. In other words such issues are capable of educational facilitation, but not of intervention.

What Can be Done to Improve Our Type of Approach?

Our crying need is to find out which aspects of our facilitation are effective, and which are ineffective - and to do something about it, purposefully.

We have experimented with structural recall situations. We have dabbled with the use of a television camera which observes a facilitator for a short time. Then it is replayed, and a participant is asked to interrupt the tape as often as is appropriate, to comment on the thoughts which were going through his or her mind at this point in time.

The technique has potential, and has already produced some interesting findings for us. But obviously it has two immediate apparent disadvantages. Only one participant at a time can really give proper feedback; and, the period of recall being somewhere of the order of eight minutes, the event must be interrupted in order to obtain constructive feedback from a participant. Nevertheless we have high hopes of the potential of this mode of enquiry, and will persist with it.

Our other priority is to find more and improved ways of determining as many as possible of the formulated needs, and of identifying unformulated needs from a variety of sources. At present this information is obtained from sources which are open to criticism on the grounds of subjectivity, and which are certainly never corroborated.

At the time of writing we have been engaged for a

mere three years in studying the status quo in continuing professional education for engineers, and in attempting to devise effective improvemens. We are satisfied that there is considerable scope for learner-centred approaches, and are conscious that their potential effectiveness will not be realised until further refinements are made in the style of working we have described. Nevertheless this appears to represent a significant advance for the participants with whom we have worked, and we have no hesitation in commending it, even in its present form.

REFERENCES

Cowan, J. (1986) "CPD -The Case for a New
    Approach", The Structural Engineer, 64A (1),
    January. 14-17.
Cowan, J. & Garry, A.M. (1986a) Report on Project
    for Self-Help Groups in Continuing Engineering
    Education, to be published by PICKUP, Department
    of Education and Science, London.
Cowan, J. & Garry, A.M. (1986b) Handbook on
    Learner-Centred Activities for CPD, to be
    published by PICKUP, Department of Education and
    Science, London.
Garry, A.M. (1985) "Tutor, Facilitator, Counsellor
    - New Demands on Course Providers", Paper
    delivered to Annual Conference of the Society for
    Research into Higher Education, December 1985.
Rogers, C.R. (1983) Freedom to Learn - for the
    1980s, Merrill, Columbus, Ohio.

AFTERWORD

"The outstanding characteristic of the
extended professional is a capacity for
autonomous, professional self-development
through systematic self-study ..."

(Stenhouse, 1975)

"Many practitioners, locked into a view of
themselves as technical experts, find
nothing in the world of practice to
occasion reflection."

(Schön, 1983)

Views of professional practice can be divided,
roughly, into two camps, consisting on the one hand
of those who see professionals as emotionally
neutral technical experts and on the other of those
who view professional practice as an arena for
personal engagement between professional and
client. In one view a professional does something
to (or for) a client; in the other a professional
works with a client. In one view personal qualities
are seen as irrelevant since what is accomplished
is seen as an outcome of the exercise of technical
expertise; in the other personal qualities are
all-important since they affect what client and
practitioner can accomplish together. In one view
possession of technical expertise confers on the
professional the right to decide a course of
action; in the other the professional draws on both
technical expertise and personal qualities to help
a client make an informed decision about a course
of action. One view gives power to the
professional; in the other power is shared between
practitioner and client. One view gives the
professional unilateral responsibility for the
client; the other views clients also as autonomous
beings capable of self-direction.

Afterword

These differing conceptions of professional practice give rise to different views of continuing professional development. One view leads to a conception of CPD as the acquisition of new technical skills; the other leads to a view of CPD as a process of self-evaluation. One view leads to a view of CPD providers as transmitters of technical knowledge; the other leads to a view of CPD designers as facilitators of reflection on practice.

This personal/instrumental distinction is the most important area of discussion for anyone working in professional development. From it flow conceptions of what CPD should be about and of the part to be played in CPD by professional institutions.

If CPD is properly the acquisition of new technical skills, then the curriculum for teaching should be based on remedying deficiencies in technical areas of practice. Such a curriculum can readily be drawn up by an outside agent – a CPD provider – on the basis of information collected on technical performance. The tasks of reviewing performance and of setting a learning agenda can both be put out to the professional's professional: the CPD provider. In this way, the relationship between professional and CPD provider mirrors that between professional and client; the CPD provider becomes a technical expert in the field of CPD.

If CPD is a process of self-monitoring and reflection on practice, then the curriculum for learning must be based on developing in the practitioner the qualities to be of help to particular clients in particular cases. Such a curriculum can only be drawn up by the practitioner in the course of a process of review of self and review of cases. The information drawn on for such a review concerns the goodness of fit between professional action and clients' needs. Clients' goals, not just objective outcomes, must therefore be acknowledged. The CPD designer has the task of supporting and encouraging the professional in this self-monitoring exercise, including seeking out such information. In this way, the relationship between professional and CPD designer mirrors that between professional and client: the CPD designer becomes a facilitator of autonomous learning choices made by an informed practitioner.

If CPD focuses on technical expertise it will be manifested in the form of programmes of instruction. A professional can demonstrate participation in CPD by attendance at such a programme and a professional institution can readily require attendance at such programmes for continued accreditation. CPD can be measured in units of time spent in such programmes, that is, time in which instruction is given. Instruction itself therefore becomes the measure for professional development; the activities of learning, and of implementing learning in practice, being less amenable to quantification, cannot be candidates for accreditation.

If CPD focuses on reflection on practice, it will be manifested in the form of enquiries conducted by the practitioner. Such enquiries may be carried out in a variety of ways: action research, reflective conversations singly or in groups, behaviour experiments, examination of records of practice, client feedback. There is no easy way of measuring the effort put into such an enquiry; the activities of learning and of implementing learning directly in practice are primary but unquantifiable; clients, however, (who find a good deal in the world of practice to occasion reflection) will notice the difference.

If CPD focuses on technical expertise, the information used to draw up a learning agenda will derive from objective measures of performance in technical areas generalised across a profession, and from knowledge of technical innovations. This information is of necessity one or two stages removed from the practice of any one individual: measures of performance are surrogates for direct examinations of practice. If CPD focuses on reflection on practice, the information used to draw up an agenda for learning will derive from subjective evaluations by practitioners of their practice, that is, directly from practice itself. The one leads to CPD programmes which loosely fit

Afterword

practice and therefore can be shared by numbers of practitioners; the other to CPD programmes which closely fit the practice of an individual practitioner or of a specific group of practitioners.

The clear-cut alternatives outlined above do not exist in isolation in the real world of professional development. This is shown by solutions described in the papers of this collection which contain features ranging along both the technical/personal dimension of practice and the instruction/facilitation dimension of CPD. Just where a particular solution falls on either of these dimensions is influenced at least in part by contextual features of the problem at hand, the possibilities or constraints intrinsic to the relationship between CPD designer and practitioner group and the brief that the CPD designer has been given. What is demonstrated here is, the sheer variety of ways of planning CPD and of CPD activities alike.

There is no one single conclusion to be drawn from the work reported here, nor is it necessary to attempt to draw one. In the final analysis professional practice must be judged by its success in each and every case. CPD must be judged by the extent to which it makes the best use of the circumstances that pertain between the CPD designer and the professional group.

The important thing is that these circumstances are evaluated and that CPD strategies are drawn up on the basis of a consideration of the gains and losses that they bring in particular contexts. It is essentially a process of reflective enquiry on the part of the designer, an enquiry conducted not on, but with, the practitioner group.

REFERENCES

Stenhouse, L. (1975) An Introduction to Curriculum
  Research and Development, Heinemann, London.
Schön, D.A. (1983) The Reflective Practitioner,
  Maurice Temple Smith, London.

NOTES ON CONTRIBUTORS

Peter A.J. Bouhuijs is an educational psychologist at the University of Limburg, Maastricht, The Netherlands, and Visiting Associate Professor in Medical Education at the University of Texas Medical Branch, Galveston, USA.

John Cowan is Professor of Engineering Education at Heriot-Watt University, Edinburgh. Recruited to the academic sphere in mid-career he has for some time concentrated on research and development which will improve the total professional learning experience, undergraduate and thereafter.

Anna Garry is a science graduate of Manchester University who came to Edinburgh, while finishing a Ph.D. on the Windscale Enquiry, to work on two projects in continuing professional development for civil engineers.

Stewart Harris, D.Phil., an expatriate of South Africa, practised an an architect for twelve years and as an educator of architects for the last eight. His education design consultancy includes the University of York, the DHSS and architectural practices amongst its clients.

Notes on Contributors

Terence Keen, Ph.D., is Project Leader, London Docklands, on secondment from Vice Principal post at Garnett College, London.

Ian Lewis is a Senior Lecturer in the Department of Education at the University of York. For the past ten years he has been actively engaged in developing MA courses which can provide a framework of support for teachers to investigate and improve aspects of their owm practice. This has led to a number of articles and papers on problems, both practical and theoretical, which this co-operation with teachers creates. In addition, he has a research interest in student perceptions of their university experience and a series of case studies of these has recently been published: The Student Experience of Higher Education (1984).

Donna S. Queeney, Ph.D., is Director, Planning Studies, Commonwealth Educational System, The Pennsylvania State University, University Park, Pennsylvania 16 802, USA.

Jill Rogers, BA, M.Phil., is currently Research Officer at the Institute of Education, University of London. Her career has been concerned with research into continuing professional education for health professionals, particularly general practitioners and nurses.

Patricia J. Sikes presently juggles two half-time jobs - as an Open University TVEI Evaluator in Barnsley, and as Secondment Tutor at the Counselling and Career Development Unit at the University of Leeds. Formerly she worked on research projects (a) at the University of East Anglia on teaching about race relations, and (b) at the Open University on teacher careers. She has a number of published works to her name, and is a co-author of Teacher Careers: Crises and Continuities (Falmer Press).

Notes on Contributors

Frankie Todd was a Research Fellow in the Institute of Advanced Architectural Studies, University of York, for the duration of the work described in this paper. She is now Co-ordinator of Continuing Education for the University of York.

Peter Woods taught history for a number of years in secondary schools. He studied education at Leeds and Bradford universities, and went to the Open University in 1972, where he is currently a Reader in Education. He has written many articles on education, edited and co-edited and -authored several books and is the author of The Divided School (1979), Sociology and the School (1983), and Inside Schools: Ethnography and Educational Research (1986), all published by Routledge and Kegan Paul.

INDEX

Index

For Product Safety Concerns and Information please contact our EU
representative GPSR@taylorandfrancis.com Taylor & Francis Verlag GmbH,
Kaufingerstraße 24, 80331 München, Germany

Printed and bound by CPI Group (UK) Ltd, Croydon, CR0 4YY
04/05/2025
01860546-0001